SHAKIRA

SHAKIRA

Katherine Krohn

Twenty-First Century Books
Minneapolis

For Cheri—who, like Shakira, has a spirit of hope

Copyright © 2008 by Katherine Krohn

All rights reserved. International copyright secured. No part of this book may be reproduced, stored in a retrieval system, or transmitted in any form or by any means—electronic, mechanical, photocopying, recording, or otherwise—without the prior written permission of Lerner Publishing Group, Inc., except for the inclusion of brief quotations in an acknowledged review.

Twenty-First Century Books
A division of Lerner Publishing Group, Inc.
241 First Avenue North
Minneapolis, MN 55401 U.S.A.

Website addresses: www.lernerbooks.com
www.biography.com

Library of Congress Cataloging-in-Publication Data

Krohn, Katherine E.
    Shakira / by Katherine Krohn.
        p.   cm. —(Biography)
    Includes bibliographical references (p. .) and index.
    ISBN 978-0-8225-7159-9 (lib. bdg. : alk. paper)
    1. Shakira—Juvenile literature. 2. Singers—Latin America—
Biography—Juvenile literature. I. Title.
ML3930.S46K76 2008
782.42164092—dc22 [B]   2007005388

Manufactured in the United States of America
1 2 3 4 5 6 – JR – 13 12 11 10 09 08

CONTENTS

96 858

Shakira performs in Bogotá, Colombia, on her 2006–2007 Oral Fixation *Tour.*

INTRODUCTION: GLOBAL SUPERSTAR

Shakira gazed out at the audience in Orlando, Florida's TD Waterhouse Centre. The performance arena was filled to capacity. She smiled broadly at the crowd. A sheer black midriff top with shiny, silver edging showed her bare stomach. Baggy black pants hung low and tight around her hips.

"Can you do one thing for me? Can you make a woman happy?" Shakira asked. Her big, brown eyes sparkled with joy. "I want you to have fun tonight!"

The crowd cheered and clapped. Some fans yelled, "I LOVE YOU!"

Shakira and her seven-piece band were on one of the final stops of her thirty-city North American *Oral Fixation* Tour. The tour was named after Shakira's 2005 back-to-back albums, *Fijación Oral, Vol. 1* (in Spanish) and *Oral Fixation, Vol. 2* (in English).

On her 2006–2007 world tour, the dynamite performer showed off her signature belly dancing in high-energy, Arab-influenced songs such as "Ojos Así" (Eyes Like Yours) and her dance hit "Whenever, Wherever." Backup dancers in bright orange costumes and rapper Wyclef Jean accompanied Shakira for her encore—"Hips Don't Lie"—the most played song in the history of radio to date. Shimmying her waist and shaking her pelvis,

Shakira made the crowd go wild. She seemed to delight in the rhythm and energy created by her body.

A reporter from the *Washington Post* saw the show during the East Coast leg of the tour. He wrote, "There was shrieking. There was hyperventilating. There was fainting. And that was just my own reaction."

MUSICAL BLEND

Shakira, who is from Colombia, is a songwriter, singer, musician, and producer. She is fluent in Spanish, English, and Portuguese. She can also speak some Italian and Arabic. Writing music and lyrics has been an important part of Shakira's life since childhood. "When she was 8 years old, she had a beautiful voice and was writing her own songs," remembers Shakira's father.
The four-foot-eleven dynamo has been performing professionally since 1990, when she was thirteen. She plays the electric guitar, drums, and even the harmonica. Her songs are inspired by her deepest feelings about life, politics, and love. "Her music is so original, and you can tell she puts a lot of thought into her lyrics—it's not just random, meaningless words," said Rosie Amorose, a thirteen-year-old Shakira fan from Oregon. Shakira often writes lyrics about her longtime love, Antonio de la Rúa, a Manhattan-based lawyer.

An accomplished belly dancer, Shakira has been belly dancing—without ever having had a lesson—since she was four years old. "I think it was something that is in my DNA," she said. Observers say that

Shakira's hips act much like another instrument. The movements of her body are as much a part of her performance as her voice. "I need to feel my music in a very physical way," Shakira told TV reporter Chris Connelly on the TV news program *20/20*. "I always say to my band, 'Hey, guys, that song is not working out. My hips, do you see? Do you see 'em moving? Do you see 'em shaking? It's not working out. So let's put a little more energy into it."

Onstage, Shakira feels powerful and confident. She doesn't show any anxiety or fear at all. Offstage, however, she is a very shy person. "I have lots of

Shakira switches to acoustic guitar during a 2003 Tour of the Mongoose concert in Caracas, Venezuela.

insecurities," she says. "I'm actually very shy." She admits, "I have the braveness to stand in front of thousands of people on a stage, but sometimes I don't feel brave enough to sing in the living room of my uncle's house in front of 20 people from my family," Shakira admits. "My heart goes racing fast. Can you believe it?"

HARD TO LABEL

Many pop stars are interpreters—they sing songs written by someone else. Shakira is different. She writes or co-writes all of her music. She also works with sound and production engineers to create the sound of each album. She insists on taking a hands-on approach to every aspect of producing an album—even helping to design the cover art.

Shakira serves as a powerful role model for Latin American girls and performers. "It's easy to see a lot of cartoon, Disney pop stars here [in Latin America]," said Gustavo Cerati, an Argentine rock musician. "It's different with her—she's involved in the production and the writing. Now a lot of women in Latin America are writing their own songs too."

Spanish singer Alejandro Sanz, who recorded the hit duet "La Tortura" (Torture) with Shakira, agrees. "She's not a puppet—she's a real musician."

Many music critics try to define Shakira's unique style. Her voice is sometimes soft and lyrical and sometimes high and pulsating. People compare her to many singers, including Tori Amos and Sheryl Crow.

Alejandro Sanz (left) joins Shakira in a live performance of "La Tortura" at the 2006 Latin Grammy Awards. Shakira took home five awards, including Song of the Year for "La Tortura."

"When Shakira's in Sheryl Crow mode, you could almost mistake her for the rockin' girl next door; then, in pelvic earthquake mode, she's Madonna with a thousand extra stomach muscles. Even her eyebrows are insanely charismatic," said Chris Willman of *Entertainment Weekly.*

Vastly different elements are evident in Shakira's music—such as hip-hop beats, new-wave synthesizers, Middle Eastern percussion, rock-and-roll guitar, and mariachi (music of Mexican street bands). "I am a fusion," says Shakira. "That's my persona. I'm a fusion between black and white, between pop and rock, between cultures—between my Lebanese father and my mother's Spanish blood, the Colombian folklore and Arab dance I love, and American music."

First arriving on the U.S. music scene with her breakthrough, crossover-to-English album, *Laundry Service* (2001), Shakira had a musical style that critics found hard to describe. At the time, some critics compared her to pop star Britney Spears. Over time music critics have discovered that Shakira is a unique individual. "[W]hen was the last time [Britney] Spears—or, for that matter, any of the current crop of divas: Christina, J. Lo, Madonna, even—lectured about politics in the middle of a concert? Or played electric guitar, or thrashed out a rhythm on the drums?" noted Nick Duerden in the music magazine *Blender.*

PASSIONATE HUMANITARIAN

Shakira sees herself as passionate. "Passion is important, obviously. Colombians are very exaggerated, and I'm exaggerated, too," she said. "I think it's a part of my romantic personality."

She is also passionate about her humanitarian causes to help people. She cares about the world. She likes to use her fame and popularity to speak up about issues that are important to her. "To be political in my country doesn't mean that you want to run for the presidency," says Shakira. "To be political simply means to have an opinion."

Shakira founded the Fundación Pies Descalzos (Bare Feet Foundation) in 1998. The organization works to build schools and better lives for the children in Latin America. In 2003 she became the

Shakira speaks at a 2006 conference in San Salvador, the capital of El Salvador. She campaigned against gang violence there.

youngest person ever appointed as a goodwill ambassador for UNICEF (the United Nations International Children's Emergency Fund).

More recently, Shakira joined forces with Colombian author Gabriel García Márquez. Together they formed the Association for Latin American Solidarity (ALAS). The foundation's fund-raising concert series will benefit children in Latin America. "In Colombia there are over 3 million kids who don't even go to school," Shakira explained. "Some think pop stars are meant to entertain, period. I don't see it that way." She added, "I think all young people have to be politically outspoken."

Shakira is wealthy, famous, and very talented. But she doesn't forget that serious problems exist in the world. "It may sound old-fashioned, but I desperately want world peace," she says.

Shakira's hometown of Barranquilla, Colombia, is a thriving industrial port town. It is home to a diverse population of Lebanese, German, Jewish, and Chinese immigrants as well as Colombians of Spanish and indigenous descent.

Chapter **ONE**

FULL OF GRACE

ON FEBRUARY 2, 1977, SHAKIRA ISABEL Mebarak Ripoll was born in Barranquilla, Colombia. This South American city is on the coast of the Caribbean Sea. The beautiful baby had big brown eyes and a short crop of dark brown hair. Shakira's name means "woman full of grace" or "grateful" in Arabic. Her father's family comes from the Middle Eastern country of Lebanon, where Arabic is the national language. Spanish is the language of Colombia and is Shakira's native tongue.

At the time she was born, Colombia had been in a civil conflict for decades. Drug crimes and armed violence plagued the country. Because of the violence, more than two million people had been displaced, losing their livelihoods and homes. Unlike some other cities in Colombia at the time, Barranquilla was fairly peaceful.

Shakira's father, William Mebarak Chadid, was born in the United States and later moved to Colombia. William is a jeweler. He also dreamed of being a writer. Shakira's mother, Nidia del Carmen Ripoll Torrado, is Colombian, of Spanish and Italian descent. Colombia has a rich culture and a diverse population—including people of Spanish, African, Italian, and Native American backgrounds. Shakira and her mother and father lived in an apartment in the suburb of El Limoncito.

Baby Shakira was the youngest of ten children. Her father has nine children from a previous marriage. Shakira's half brothers, William, Alberto, Edward, Moises, Tonino, and Robin, and her half sisters, Ana, Lucy, and Patricia, lived with their mother a few blocks away. Shakira's siblings were thrilled to have a new baby sister. They showered little Shakira with attention.

SAD EYES

When Shakira was only two, her family suffered a huge loss. Her oldest brother, William, was killed when a drunk driver hit him on his motorcycle. Shakira's earliest memory is of the police coming to the door and telling her family that eighteen-year-old William was dead. "That's actually my first memory of my life," Shakira later said. "I remember the exact moment when my parents got the news."

It's All in a Name

n many Spanish-speaking countries, people have double last names. The names represent both sides of their families. The first is their father's last name. The second is their mother's name. Women don't change their names after marriage, but their children get new blended last names.

For example, Shakira's mother's name is Nidia del Carmen Ripoll Torrado. Ripoll is her father's name, and Torrado is her mother's name. William Mebarak Chadid is Shakira's father. Mebarak is his father's name. Chadid is his mother's name. Shakira's first name is followed first by her father's family name, Mebarak, and then her mother's family name, Ripoll. People are usually called by the first of their two last names.

The family was grief stricken by the tragedy. Her father had an especially hard time with the loss. For years, he wore dark glasses to cover his sad eyes.

Child Prodigy

Shakira was a creative and highly intelligent child. At four she wrote her first poem, "La Rose de Cristal" (The Crystal Rose). The same year, Shakira's family had dinner at a Middle Eastern restaurant. Tiny Shakira heard the *tek-tek-tek* beat of the *doumbek,* the Middle Eastern drum that traditionally provides rhythms for belly dancing. She listened to the music, and she couldn't sit still. Her hips began to move, and she sprang from her chair in the restaurant. She twirled around and shook her hips to the music. Shakira delighted her family and friends—and amazed the other restaurant customers—by doing a belly dance in front of the whole restaurant. No one had ever taught Shakira how to belly dance. "Her belly dance show was amazing," said family friend Kathy Kopp. "Because she was so good, and she was so tiny. And she was so cute."

She loved performing and having people look at her. She especially liked to share the joy she felt inside—and to see people get happier when she performed. "I fell in love with the sensation of being on stage," Shakira said later. "Right there, right then. It was all I could dream of."

Because she had so many brothers and sisters, and she was the youngest child in her family, she got a great deal of attention. Her siblings got a kick out of seeing little Shakira sing and dance. "That made me an attention-addicted person," Shakira said, about having so many adoring siblings. "If you ever hear about a rehab clinic for attention-dependent people, let me know, please," she later told a reporter.

Shakira gave belly dancing performances at family gatherings. She even performed for her teachers and classmates. The Ripoll family is Roman Catholic, like most Colombians. Shakira attended La Enseñanza de

Barranquilla (the School of Barranquilla), a traditional Catholic school. Many of her teachers were nuns. The teachers didn't just teach academic subjects like science and math. They provided lessons about the Catholic religion and how to live your life.

The nuns appreciated Shakira's talent and encouraged her interest in belly dancing. "Fridays were special and I performed for the whole school each week," Shakira remembered. "The nuns weren't shocked. They considered it an art." She added, "I drove my classmates crazy."

Shakira also liked to play with her friends. Her favorite game was one that she made up. "We pretended to be an organization searching for petroleum," she recalled. (Petroleum, or oil, is one of Colombia's biggest money-making resources.) "I was, of course, the chief."

A BLEATING GOAT

Besides dancing, young Shakira loved to sing. In the second grade, she auditioned to be in the school choir. Unfortunately, the teacher didn't like Shakira's voice. He thought her voice had too much vibrato (pulsing or throbbing in a singer's voice) and would overpower the other voices in the choir. She was crushed when the teacher told Shakira that she couldn't be in the chorus. To make things worse, Shakira's classmates teased her. They told her that she sounded like a bleating goat.

The discouragement made Shakira think about never singing again. But then she changed her mind. Why should she let anybody else stop her from doing what she loved to do—sing?

The young girl also liked to write. "My dad was a writer and to see him always in front of a typewriter gave me the inspiration to write," Shakira later said. "He was my idol, my hero. I wanted to be just like him."

When she was seven, Shakira prayed for a typewriter. On her eighth birthday, her wish came true. She was thrilled when she opened a big box and saw that one of her aunts had given her a shiny new typewriter.

Shakira's parents noticed their daughter's early interest in writing and thought she might one day be a great author. At first her parents didn't know what she was writing on her typewriter. It turned out that she was mostly writing lyrics to songs.

One day Shakira went up to her father with a piece of typing paper in her hand. "Daddy, I want you to listen to this song," said Shakira. She looked down at the piece of paper and sang the words. She called the song "Tus Gafas Oscuras" (Your Dark Sunglasses).

Shakira's father was deeply moved by the words. "From the moment I lost my elder child, I hid my grief behind the dark glasses," William later said, "so I realized she was making a connection with the glasses I wore."

In fact, Shakira later said that the song was inspired by an imaginary boyfriend. "Because at that time, I did not have a boyfriend, I was eight years old," she said, so she made one up "Even when I was a little child, the subjects of my songs were romantic. But I took the sunglasses as a motif. Because, you know, children just take advantage of the small realities, the few things that happen in their lives, because their world is very small."

REALITY CHECK

When Shakira was eight, her family's jewelry business went bankrupt. At first she didn't understand what was happening. While her father figured out what to do next, he sent Shakira and her mother to live with friends in Los Angeles, California, for three months. When they returned, Shakira noticed changes around the house. Her father had sold some of their things to raise money. The air conditioner was gone, and their big color TV was gone too. A small, black-and-white TV had taken its place. Shakira's large, fancy bed was gone. Instead, her father had gotten her a small, plain bed.

Shakira was not happy. She wanted her bed back! She missed the large color TV. She wanted her life to be the way it was before her family went bankrupt. "I was so upset," Shakira later said. "So my parents took me to the park to see the orphans who were sniffing glue to survive their hunger, and they said, 'See, there are people who are going through worse situations than you.'"

She was deeply affected by the sight of the hungry children. Like thousands of children in Colombia, the

In the late 1970s, as in the twenty-first century, many Colombian children lived in terrible poverty. These children carried bricks at a building site instead of attending school. They worked long hours to make enough money to survive.

orphans had lost their parents and homes through violence. Shakira's own situation didn't seem so bad anymore. At least she had loving parents and a roof over her head, she thought. At that moment, she promised herself something important. If she ever reached her dream of being a famous, wealthy performer, she would do something to help those children.

FUTURE PLAN

Though Shakira's family had less money than before, their home life was rich. Meals were very important to her family. Mealtime was for sharing thoughts, catching up on one another's day, and discussing ideas. Her parents encouraged her to think deeply about many subjects.

"My dad always liked to have interesting conversation at the table," Shakira remembered. "He liked to try to teach us about literature, he was always very attracted to politics, and he would want to find out what we thought about different things. He always made it interesting."

Her father was a bit of a dreamer. He had one foot in the future, and his mind was always open to new and creative ideas. On the other hand, her mother was more down-to-earth and practical.

Shakira believes she is like both of her parents. Sometimes she is practical like her mom. But she is a dreamer like her dad. "I thank God that I am a product of my parents," Shakira said, and that "they infected me with their intelligence and energy for life, with their thirst for knowledge and their love."

The family loved music, and a wide variety of music could be heard on the record player in Shakira's house. Her parents enjoyed bolero (a Spanish dance) music and traditional Colombian music, such as *cumbia* (fast-paced salsa) music. Shakira's dad also liked to listen to Middle Eastern music. These musical styles influenced Shakira's songwriting.

Shakira's parents knew that she was gifted. They wanted to encourage her interest in music and performance. For Christmas they gave her a guitar. And to help her gain poise and confidence, they enrolled her in a modeling school in Barranquilla. Meanwhile, Shakira continued to practice her singing, and when she was ten, she entered a talent contest at a local TV station. She wore a sequined cowgirl outfit and sang and danced. She was thrilled when she won the first-place prize, a bicycle.

Ten-year-old Shakira choreographed dance routines to accompany her music, and she enlisted two of her classmates from modeling school to perform with her. The children worked as a variety song-and-dance troupe, performing in small towns in the area. "By the time I was 10, I had already made a decision about my future," said Shakira. "I knew that I wanted to pursue a musical career, to sing for the rest of my life."

FIRST LOVE

When Shakira was twelve, she met the boy who became her first boyfriend. But her father didn't approve. He thought that she was much too young to have a boyfriend. But Shakira had made up her mind. "Listen, I like this guy. I'm gonna be his girlfriend whether you like it or not," she told her father. "Do you want to know about my life? Or do you want me to hide what I do?"

Shakira's father loved his daughter and wanted to have an honest relationship with her. "Okay, I want to know about it," he decided. William knew that

Shakira had a good head on her shoulders and that he could trust her. She didn't take drugs or drink alcohol, and she wasn't rebellious.

"I was always a good girl," she later said. Instead of partying, young Shakira wrote songs. She worked out songs on her guitar and typed lyrics on her typewriter.

"The first songs I wrote were dramatic love songs," said Shakira. "A 13-year-old girl singing love and hate songs was a little radical. Some people thought I was a 30-year-old woman. And there were local critics who weren't into the idea that a young girl was singing such dramatic love songs."

"DREAMING OF A RECORD CONTRACT"

Shakira's favorite band was Led Zeppelin, the British rock band that created hits such as "Stairway to Heaven" and "Whole Lotta Love." She also liked the Beatles, Nirvana, the Cure, and the Police. Shakira liked heavy metal too, especially the band Metallica. She couldn't understand a word of English at the time. "The lyrics were all *blah blah blah blah,*" she later recalled.

At thirteen Shakira especially liked Depeche Mode, an electronic rock band from Great Britain. One day she was listening to the band's song, "Enjoy the Silence." She noticed that she was not only hearing the music but also feeling the music in her body. She said to her mother, "Every time I hear that guitar riff [a rhythmic musical phrase] I feel this weird thing in my stomach."

MUSICAL INSPIRATIONS

Since she was a teenager, Shakira has loved a wide range of music. Musicians such as Led Zeppelin, Nirvana, the Cure, and the Police inspired her to become a rock musician. "People like Tracy Chapman showed me that there was a way to make good lyrics in English," said Shakira. Bob Dylan and Leonard Cohen influenced Shakira's songwriting too. She also admires jazz musicians Ella Fitzgerald and Billie Holiday.

As a young girl, Shakira listened to disco legend Donna Summer—her mother had her album *Bad Girls*. "And I loved that music. I still do. You know, that is the kind of music that never dies, that will never sound dated. You can still listen to it and feel like dancing."

The British band Led Zeppelin is one of Shakira's favorites. The band formed in London in 1968.

"I still feel it," Shakira later said, of the guitar riff. "That's how I discovered there was something in the electric guitar that was really powerful." She decided then that she, too, wanted to make that kind of music. She wanted to be a rock musician.

On the weekends, Shakira continued to perform with her variety troupe. She also continued to write songs. "Always I was dreaming of a record contract. From 10 to 13 it was all I could think of," she later said. "Nobody could say I didn't try."

One day in 1990, Shakira was performing at a local talent contest in Barranquilla. The thirteen-year-old girl didn't know it, but someone was in the audience who would change her life. Monica Ariza, a local theater producer, was watching Shakira's act. Ariza saw something special in Shakira—both extraordinary talent and something you can't teach or buy—charisma. After the show, Ariza approached Shakira and her parents. She told them that an executive from Sony Records, Ciro Vargas, would soon be passing through Barranquilla. Shakira should audition for him, she said. Ariza had a hunch that this singer might be just the kind of fresh, new talent that would interest Vargas.

In 1994 Shakira chased her dreams of success to Bogotá, the capital of Colombia.

Chapter **TWO**

MAGIC

SHAKIRA AUDITIONED FOR CIRO VARGAS IN THE lobby of the hotel where he was staying. She stood in front of him and sang a cappella (without instruments). Her proud parents stood by and watched. Vargas was impressed. A few days later, he took his business colleagues to a public performance that featured Shakira. There the teenager showed off her singing and belly dancing moves. The bosses at Sony were impressed. They signed young Shakira—who had never had a formal music lesson in her life—to a three-album contract. She was thrilled. She was only thirteen, and her dream of being a professional singer had already come true!

In 1991 Sony released *Magia* (Magic), a collection of heartfelt love songs. "Ever since her first album, recorded when she was 13, her songs have described relationships as a wonderful agony and love as a spell that turns the bearer into *un perro faldero*, a tag-along dog," wrote Rob Tannenbaum in *Blender*.

The album was a success locally, but Sony wasn't satisfied. They had hoped for bigger sales. Shakira didn't get discouraged. She knew in her heart that she was meant to be a songwriter and singer. She kept writing songs and taking steps toward her dream.

Shakira worked hard, and she worked mostly on her own at first. "When I started I didn't have a make-up artist, a hairdresser, an assistant, a marketing plan," she said. "I started without having anything, just laying one brick after the other, under the sun, by myself."

Shakira spent long hours in the studio, working on arrangements with record producers and musicians. She soon learned that her youth stood in the way of her success. "The issue I had to deal with at the beginning of my career was not my sex but my age— because I was a child in a world of adults. So I had to make my opinions be taken into account."

Unfortunately, despite her attempts to defend her creative vision, Shakira's second album was more her producer's vision than her own. In 1993 *Peligro* (Danger) was released.

Peligro did not do well in the stores, but still Shakira didn't get discouraged. "There was no doubt for me, ever," she said years later. "Call it a premonition, call it an instinct. I was born to do this, to connect with a wide audience. The calling I have is the same reason why a dog barks. I always knew I would be a big performer and a public figure."

At fifteen Shakira got some bad news. Sony had decided not to go ahead with her third album. Instead of giving up, the teenager pushed forward. She entered a popular Latin American singing contest in Viña del Mar, Chile, and won second place.

Soon Shakira graduated from high school. Instead of going to college, she wanted to focus on her career. She knew she needed to move to a larger city if she really wanted to get her career further off the ground. But she was too young to move by herself. She talked her mother into going with her to Bogotá, Colombia. The two of them rented a room in a boardinghouse, and soon Shakira began to audition for local productions.

SOAP STAR

In 1996 Shakira landed a role in a Colombian TV show, *El Oasis* (The Oasis). The show was a *telenovela*, a very popular TV miniseries in Latin America. Telenovelas are like soap operas, but they air in prime-time evening slots. In her role, Shakira played a wealthy girl named Luisa Maria who was in a rocky romance. She also sang the show's theme song "Lo Mío" (What's Mine).

Shakira liked acting in *El Oasis*, but she really just wanted to make music. Her heart wasn't in being an actress—and it showed. "I was a really bad actress, I must confess," she later said. She is embarrassed to watch old episodes of the series, because she thinks she overacted in her role.

Nineteen-year-old Shakira's plan was to keep writing songs. When she was ready, she figured, she would return to Sony and ask Vargas to fulfill her contract. She hadn't given up on making a third album.

While appearing in *El Oasis,* Shakira started dating handsome Puerto Rican soap opera star Osvaldo Ríos. Tabloid newspapers followed every move of the glamorous, young couple. Eventually, their rocky romance came to an end. But the painful relationship fueled Shakira's songwriting.

SOARING SUCCESS

While still acting in *El Oasis,* Shakira penned the song "¿Dónde Estás Corazón?" (Where Are You, Honey?). In the song, she expressed her desire to

Shakira dated costar Osvaldo Ríos while she acted in El Oasis. *Soap opera fans loved reading about the behind-the-scenes romance as much as they enjoyed watching the show itself.*

meet the love of her life. A rock-music collection featured the song, and it quickly became a major hit in Latin America.

Impressed by Shakira's hit record, the executives at Sony Music Latin America wanted to work with the singer again. Fortunately, Shakira had written several songs and had enough material for a third album. But this time, she wanted to have more creative control on the album's production. The Sony bosses agreed.

In 1996 Shakira's album *Pies Descalzos* (Bare Feet) was released. One song on the album, "Estoy Aquí" (I'm Here), was especially popular with music fans. The song was soon a hit. The album skyrocketed to number one in Latin America, where people got to know the name Shakira. The record rose to number one in eight countries and went platinum (sold over one million copies) in the United States. Nineteen-year-old Shakira's third album and first international release had propelled her to fame.

Miami Bound

In 1997 Shakira made an important decision. At twenty years old, she figured it was the right time to move to the United States. There she knew that she would have more opportunities to achieve her dream of being an international performer. So Shakira and her parents packed their bags and moved to Miami, Florida. Using money from her *Pies Descalzos* success, Shakira bought a house near the ocean for her family.

Sony arranged a concert tour of North America to promote Shakira's album. She was thrilled when she was also scheduled to give a concert in Barranquilla—her first hometown appearance since becoming famous.

TRAGEDY FALLS

Backstage in Barranquilla, Shakira's heart raced. She was happy and excited to perform for her fellow Colombians. She knew the stadium was filled with many friends and family members.

But the day turned tragic when fifty thousand fans rushed into the stadium to see Shakira. The surge of fans was so strong that security couldn't control them. Two people were trampled to death.

Shakira was devastated. Her dream was only to bring music and joy to her people, not tragedy. She left the stage and went into seclusion. She felt devastated and unable to sing. "She thought that it was her fault those people had died because they went to see her sing," said Shakira's brother Tonino. "She thought about abandoning her career, she didn't want to go on singing."

Friends and family assured Shakira that the tragedy was not her fault. Still shook up by the incident, she pulled together her strength to go on. She knew she was meant to sing.

MEETING THE ESTEFANS

Soon Shakira met a famous record producer who would help her achieve her dreams to be an international success. Emilio Estefan had helped build the career of his famous wife, Cuban-American pop star Gloria Estefan.

Emilio Estefan saw something special in Shakira. He thought that she had the potential to be a crossover star. Crossover stars are huge successes not only in their home country but across the world.

Working under the production guidance of Emilio, Shakira put together a new album. Something disturbing happened during production. Shakira's luggage, including a suitcase that held all of her lyrics, was stolen at an airport. The songwriter was very upset. She hadn't made backup copies of her lyrics. Unwilling to give up, she wrote a whole new set of lyrics that she liked even better. The theft inspired Shakira to write a new song too—the title song of her new album.

In 1998 *¿Dónde Están los Ladrones?* (Where Are the Thieves?) was released. The album soared to the number-one spot on *Billboard*'s Latin Album Chart. It stayed there for eleven weeks. The album was a success in both the United States and Latin America. One track on the album, "Ciega, Sordomuda" (Blind, Deaf, and Mute), reached the number-one spot on *Billboard* magazine's Hot Latin Tracks chart for four weeks in 1998. The song, about love being blind, reached the top ten in the charts of every single country in Latin America.

Gloria Estefan had walked the very road that Shakira was on, years earlier. She had special advice

Gloria and Emilio Estefan attend a Billboard Latin Music Awards ceremony in Miami Beach, Florida, in the late 1990s.

for Shakira about her newly found fame. "It gets bigger, but it doesn't get better, so you'd better enjoy it now," said Gloria.

More and more people around the world were discovering Shakira. Fans said they found her songs deeply moving and beautiful. Others commented that Shakira's songs made them weep. The lyrics, often about love and heartache, resonated with events in their own lives. Some people found Shakira's voice to be unusual but appealing.

THE ESTEFANS

loria Estefan is known as the Queen of Latin Pop and is the largest Latin American crossover success in the world. Her husband, Emilio, is credited with launching Gloria's career to superstardom.

One evening in 1975, a little-known band called the Miami Latin Boys was performing at a large wedding in Florida. Band member Emilio Estefan, a Cuban American, asked Cuban-born Gloria Fajardo to sing a number with the band. Everyone loved Gloria's powerful, velvety voice. The band asked Gloria to become a member. She and Emilio married in 1978.

Emilio guided the band, now called the Miami Sound Machine, to international success. Songs such as "Get on Your Feet" and "Conga" became number-one hits. In 1989 Emilio left the Miami Sound Machine to become a full-time manager, and the band changed its name to Gloria Estefan and the Miami Sound Machine. They were riding a thrilling wave of international success. But in 1990, a traffic accident broke Gloria's spine. With fierce determination, physical therapy, and faith, Gloria eventually fully recovered.

Like their friend Shakira, Emilio and Gloria's humanitarian work is very important to them. In 1997 the Estefans formed the Gloria Estefan Foundation to provide education and financial support to children. The Estefans live on the beautiful Star Island near Miami. They have two grown children. Emilio is responsible for launching the careers of several top Latin American performers, including Ricky Martin, Jon Secada—and Shakira. Besides being a five-time Grammy Award winner, Gloria is also a best-selling author of two children's picture books.

In 1998 Shakira was happy to be able to fulfill another dream. She founded an organization to help the children of Colombia. She named it the Fundación Pies Descalzos (Bare Feet Foundation) after her 1996 album. Together with a team of caring people, Shakira planned to offer food and hope to needy families. She also planned to build schools all over Colombia.

A NEW FRIENDSHIP

World-famous Colombian author Gabriel García Márquez interviewed Shakira in Spanish for a magazine article in 1999. The seventy-one-year-old Márquez had won the Nobel Prize for his book *One Hundred Years of Solitude* in 1982. Márquez writes in a style known as magic realism, popular in Latin America.

Gabriel García Márquez, also known as Gabo, was born in Colombia in 1928. He later attended boarding school in Shakira's hometown, Barranquilla. The two are good friends.

Interestingly, his grandmother inspired his writing voice. As a boy, Márquez's grandmother would tell him fanciful tales that involved supernatural events. He noticed that his grandmother never expressed disbelief in the stories she told. Instead, she always kept a straight face—no matter how wild the tale. As an author, Márquez attempts to write novels in the same way that his grandmother told stories.

Márquez was impressed with Shakira, who is also extremely imaginative. He said, "Shakira's music has a personal stamp that doesn't look like anyone else's and no one can sing or dance like her, at whatever age, with such an innocent sensuality, one that seems to be of her own invention."

After meeting, Márquez and Shakira realized they had a lot in common, and they became good friends. They began to plan to work together on major projects benefiting the children of Colombia.

LEARNING ENGLISH

Shakira wanted to help as many people as she could, not just in her homeland of Colombia but all over the world. The only way to do that, she figured, was to reach a broader audience with her music. Her record company had the same idea.

"When my record company asked, 'Do you want to make an album in English?' I said yeah, right then. But then I realized I was in trouble," said Shakira. "I accepted the challenge, but I didn't know if I

Shakira's parents joined her at the 1999 Billboard Latin Music Awards, where she won the award for Best Female Pop Artist.

would be able to reach that goal." Shakira didn't know any English. And not only would she have to master a new language, she'd have to write song lyrics in English too.

Emilio Estefan, Shakira's manager, encouraged her to learn English. He knew that if she could sing in English, she would be a superstar in the United States and other English-speaking countries. He hired a private tutor in Miami for her. The teacher worked with her for several months. But, to understand songwriting in English, she would have to learn more than just the basics of the English language. She studied the lyrics of artists she admired, such as Bob Dylan, Leonard Cohen, and Tracy Chapman. She also read the works of famous poets, such as Walt Whitman. She found that reading the daily newspaper helped too.

But sometimes Shakira felt discouraged. "I was born in Spanish, I grew up in Spanish, I love in Spanish, I get angry in Spanish," she said. "When I realized the implications of having to write my next album in English, I thought, 'How did I get myself into this?'"

Gloria Estefan had taken Shakira under her wing. Years earlier, she too had to learn English and record music in a new language. Estefan believed in the younger singer and encouraged her to push on. "She told me, 'You can do it. Come on! You just need to practice a little more,'" Shakira said.

"At first it seemed impossible," said Shakira. "And then it turned more and more passionate. As a composer, it was a great adventure." She considered learning English the biggest challenge of her life. "Learning a new language enlarged my world," said Shakira. "There was some suffering, but many rewards."

Shakira performs one of her famous belly dances at the launch party of her 2001 album Laundry Service.

Chapter **THREE**

LAUNDRY SERVICE

ONE EVENING IN APRIL **1999, A WELL-KNOWN** talent manager, Freddy DeMann, was sitting at home with his wife. They were watching the American Latin Music Awards (ALMA). On the show, Shakira performed "Come to My Window" with famous rock star Melissa Etheridge. Shakira had recently dyed her hair red. She wore a black turtleneck sweater and black pants. Though English was a new language for her, she sang the duet with confidence and passion.

"I said to my wife, 'Who is that girl?'" DeMann later said. "The next day I called the producer of the show. He said her name was Shakira. I'd never heard of her. But I knew she was going to be a star."

Freddy DeMann and Madonna founded Maverick Records in 1991. He has also produced movies and Broadway shows.

DeMann soon discovered that Shakira had a manager. He bided his time. Six months later, he flew to Miami to meet her. "When she walked in the room, I nearly had a heart attack, she had that much presence," said DeMann.

Shakira liked DeMann too. She decided to hire him as her new manager. She knew that DeMann had managed the careers of many superstars, including Madonna and Michael Jackson. And, while Emilio Estefan was a good manager, Shakira wasn't his only priority.

"Emilio has a lot of other projects," Shakira said. "We always said that at some moment there would be a transition to another manager who could focus on my career 100 percent. But he's still there for me."

Because DeMann had managed Madonna, some people thought that he would try to turn Shakira into "the next

Madonna" or an even bigger star. But his new musician didn't just want to be a superstar. "My dream is to transcend, to break cultural barriers," said Shakira, who critics predict will one day be a superstar in the same league as stars such as Madonna. "If I thought of being bigger than Madonna, then my dreams would turn into plain ambition and would stop being dreams."

A LOVE MAP

With her English dictionary in hand, Shakira set to work on her next project—her first English-language album. She believes that while working on the album, she also "designed" the man of her dreams—the man she hoped to one day meet and fall in love with. Shakira had had several boyfriends. But none of her relationships had lasted. "I had experiences of bad boys who did not tell the truth," Shakira explained. "Truth is important to me. I always say that in my town the people do not lie and that's what I was looking for in life. So while recording the album I designed the man of my life in my head."

"I made a love map in my head. I had to make sure I wasn't designing anything that had been made before, you see," said Shakira. "I didn't want to design anything similar to my past. My relationships in the past were not the best things for my future."

While working on the album, Shakira continued to perform. In 2000 her manager booked her for concerts in several cities around the world. One of her stops was Argentina. As it would turn out, Shakira's "love map" had led her to the right place.

A HANDSOME STRANGER

One evening in Argentina, Shakira and her family dined at a restaurant. Across the room, she saw a young man looking at her. The man had tousled brown hair, full lips, and a husky build. "I looked at him from a distance and I said, oh, my God, how handsome this guy is." Shakira later said, "It was love at first sight, for both of us."

While she ate, Shakira continued to share shy glances with the handsome stranger. She wanted to see him closer up, so she excused herself to go to the bathroom. "I never went to the bathroom so many times in a night," she later said. "But nothing happened."

Shakira didn't know it at the time, but the man who had caught her eye was very well known in Argentina. He was Antonio de la Rúa. His father is Fernando de la Rúa, the president of Argentina at the time. Antonio was one of Argentina's most eligible bachelors.

Antonio had recognized Shakira—after all, she was a famous performer. He had wanted to come to her table and talk to her, but he didn't know how.

Shakira returned to Miami, but she told her manager she wanted to do another concert in Argentina. "I wasn't supposed to go back, but I said, I have to go back, because there's something I have to complete," she said.

Not knowing what her unfinished business was exactly, Shakira returned to Argentina. Her intuition was correct. Antonio and his brother attended Shakira's concert in Buenos Aires, the capital of Argentina. Afterward they met with the performer. Shakira liked Antonio, but she didn't realize who he was. "I didn't associate him with the night when we first met. I just felt a certain familiarity with him. Then I continued with my tour, and then I came back to Argentina a month later.

"And I saw him again, and we went to have dinner, and then I realized, oh, my God, this is the same guy I saw in that restaurant in January. And forget about it. After that, we never separated." Shakira knew she had met the love of her life.

Shakira and Antonio de la Rúa soon became the most photographed couple in Latin America. Photographers from Spanish-speaking tabloid newspapers followed them everywhere. The public was fascinated by their romance.

The relationship inspired Shakira to write songs—especially love songs. Later in 2000, she released a concert album, *MTV Unplugged*. A Music Television "unplugged" album is made without any electric instruments. Shakira wrote all the music and lyrics for the album. She also played the harmonica on the album, as well as the acoustic guitar on "Inevitable."

Three main musicians backed up Shakira. Tim Mitchell performed on guitar, Luis Fernando Ochoa

Shakira and Antonio de la Rúa attend a release party and live performance by Rolling Stones front man Mick Jagger.

on guitar and keyboards, and Brendan Buckley on drums. In the past, Mitchell had played lead guitar with several top musicians, including Gloria Estefan, rocker Bob Seger, and Jon Secada. Many musicians contributed to the project, playing a variety of instruments including the lap steel guitar, mandolin, piano, and the bouzouki (a pear-shaped, stringed instrument with a long neck). Even a traditional Mexican mariachi band played on "Ciega, Sordomuda." *MTV Unplugged* won several awards including a Grammy Award for Best Latin Pop Album. It also won a *Billboard* Latin Music Award for Best Latin Album.

"ONE MORE BLONDE IN THE WORLD"

Shakira's natural hair color is dark brown. For several
months, she enjoyed being a redhead. "But every time
I went to the beach, the water would become pink
and my hair would fade to orange. So now there's one
more blonde in the world."

Some people in the Latin American community did
not like it that Shakira dyed her hair blonde. They
thought she was trying to hide the fact that she was
Hispanic.

"I know my Latin people find this difficult. And I want
[my success] to be good news to my country. But it's typ-
ical that when you see somebody who is so close to you
growing, you feel that the very word 'growing' is synony-
mous with leaving," Shakira told *Teen People*.

"My Latin market is as important, or more [so], than
others," said Shakira. "It's not that I'm abandoning one
territory for the other. On the contrary: I'm expanding."

Chicago Tribune reporter Teresa Puente disagrees.
She believes that when Hispanic pop stars such as
Jennifer Lopez and Shakira lighten their hair, it sends
a bad message to all women of color. "Some think it
is better to have lighter hair, eyes and skin color,"
wrote Puente. "This desire to look 'whiter' . . . has
resulted in steady sales of cream bleaches, colored
contacts and hair dye. Throughout history, women of
all cultures have gone to extremes to change their
appearance to fit popular notions of what is beautiful
in their male-dominated worlds."

But Shakira simply saw her dye job as a fashion statement. "I have always been proud of my roots," she said, defending her choice. "Like most women, I like changing my look."

CROSSOVER SUCCESS

In 2001 Shakira released her much-awaited crossover album, *Laundry Service*. It featured nine songs in English and four in Spanish. "It was a little bit of a struggle in the beginning to produce the album in English," Shakira told the press. "It was a challenge to write in

Shakira performs at Tower Records on Sunset Boulevard in Los Angeles, California. Live performances across the United States helped make Laundry Service a crossover hit.

English for the first time. But, like with everything, the first step is the most difficult, and then the second comes naturally. I've already walked a whole block."

Many people from the press asked Shakira how she chose the name for her new album. "The reason I named it *Laundry Service* is because I've spent the year dedicated to my two great passions: love and music," she said. "Those two elements are like soap and water. It was a deep cleansing, almost like being reborn."

Shakira designed the cover art for *Laundry Service* too. The album cover features a close-up of a blonde, bare-skinned Shakira with "Laundry Service" and a star tattooed on her upper right arm.

The album sold 3.5 million copies in the United States. The singles "Whenever, Wherever" and "Underneath Your Clothes" became hits. Shakira's video version of "Whenever, Wherever" was a favorite on MTV. Important executives in the record and TV business were excited about her potential. Because her music had a unique, diverse sound, the music bosses knew Shakira wouldn't be a one-hit wonder. She had staying power.

Shakira wrote "Whenever, Wherever" about her relationship with Antonio, which is often long-distance. "Those nice love songs? Those are dedicated and inspired by him," she admitted. She points out, however, that not all the songs she wrote are about Antonio. "[T]here are dramatic songs that I wrote before I met him. Not everything [about love] is pink and filled with sparkles."

Music critics admired the uniqueness of Shakira's musical style. Rob Tannenbaum in *Blender* wrote that *Laundry Service* "mixed synthesizers with acoustic guitars—plus trashy guitar riffs, big, frisky rock beats and Shakira's throaty, Middle Eastern roar—in an audacious, mongrelized way that felt both instantly familiar and entirely inventive."

On the album, Shakira experiments with several musical forms, including tango (dramatic, sexy Argentine dance music), '80s new-wave, disco, and Middle Eastern music. "Somehow I'm a fusion of all of those passions and my music is a fusion of the elements that I can make coexist in the same place, in one song," she explained.

Shakira translated some of her English songs to Spanish. The Spanish version of "Whenever, Wherever," called "Suerte" (meaning "luck"), was number one in the *Billboard* Hot Latin Tracks chart for five weeks.

Many music critics compared Shakira to Britney Spears. At the time, Spears was a fresh, new teen idol at the height of pop fame. "Nothing wrong with Britney," said Shakira. "She's a great artist and very beautiful, but I was pretty surprised to be compared to her in America and Britain. But I think that's because there isn't a full understanding of my musical proposal here. That's a matter of time though."

In some ways, Shakira resembled Britney in her early days. They are both petite and have long, blonde hair, a big smile, and bright eyes. Onstage, they are full of energy and charismatic. "But as soon as [Shakira] opens her mouth," wrote the *Observer* of London, "she slips into gear and motors powerfully past Britney's breathy bump 'n' grind. This song that she's singing, 'Underneath Your Clothes,' may be slightly kooky pop-rock, but it's sung by someone with the range of an operatic diva."

Some reviewers criticized Shakira's voice. A reporter from the *Dallas Morning News* commented that on some songs "her quavering, high-pitched voice can grate on the nerves."

Music critics compared Shakira to other performers of the time, especially women with unique voices and vocal styles, such as Tori Amos and Björk. Several reviewers compared Shakira's voice to Alanis Morissette, whose singing voice is often guttural (from the back of the throat). Shakira considers the comparison a compliment. "She's one of the best female singer-songwriters of this decade," she said of Morissette. "I have a great admiration for her. If I ever met her, I know that we would have a lot to talk about. She's one of those people who I feel I have things in common with."

The critics didn't realize that Shakira was one of a kind. She couldn't be compared to anyone.

SHE GETS BUTTERFLIES

In 2001 Shakira became a spokeswoman for Pepsi. She appeared in several TV commercials released in both English and Spanish. In one commercial, Shakira is featured as a life-sized cardboard cutout figure in a convenience store. The cardboard Shakira springs to life and dances with a nerdy, young convenience store clerk. She also performed as a musical guest on several television programs such as *The Rosie O'Donnell Show, The Tonight Show with Jay Leno,* and *Saturday Night Live.*

Shakira puts her heart into every performance, even when she sings the same songs night after night. And she always gets butterflies in her stomach before she goes onstage. "I feel the exact thing before I sing on *Saturday Night Live* as when I sang on a very small TV show in Colombia," she told *Teen People.* "Before the first singing contest I ever participated in, I felt the same nervousness I feel now."

SHAKIRA RECORDS PULLED OFF SHELVES

In December 2001, Antonio de la Rúa's father resigned from office in Argentina. He left the country in a political and economic crisis. Antonio had acted as a political adviser to his father. After the resignation, some people in Latin America didn't approve of Shakira and Antonio's relationship anymore.

The Argentina branch of Tower Records pulled all of Shakira's albums off the shelves in protest, because Antonio de la Rúa was featured in her video for the song "Debajo de Tu Ropa" (Underneath Your Clothes). On March 4, 2002, Tower Records Argentina announced it was banning sales of her records. Argentine reporters were angry that Antonio, linked with his father politi-

On December 20, 2001, President Fernando de la Rúa addressed Argentina from the Government House in Buenos Aires. He offered to compromise with the political parties that opposed him, but they refused. He resigned from the presidency that evening.

cally, would appear in a rock video during a time of national crisis.

After the incident, Antonio, like his father, kept a low profile. He avoided photographers and the press as much as possible. Shakira refused to comment to the press about the political situation. But she insisted that she and Antonio remained very committed to each other.

Another controversial issue faced Shakira in 2002. In late 2001, Shakira had modeled for Delia's, a line of hip teen fashions. Maria Arriaga, a Mexican immigrant, blew the whistle on a garment factory that made clothes for Delia's. She explained to the U.S. Labor Department that the factory, in Brooklyn, New York, had "sweatshop conditions." They had forced employees to work overtime, without pay, for years.

When Shakira learned of this, she released a statement to the press, saying, "I support the fight for just wages." She added, "I was unaware of the dispute in Brooklyn. I would never knowingly wear clothes or support any company who produced clothing with alleged wage and labor violations."

Shakira and Delia's reportedly hadn't been aware of the labor abuses in the Brooklyn factory. A lawyer for the factory workers, Steven Jenkins, said, "While it's good to know that Shakira is against sweatshops, it's important that people do more to assure clothing is made under just and humane conditions."

Despite controversy in the Latin American community, Shakira remained popular with her fans. In October 2002, Music Television presented the very first MTV Latin American Music Awards, in Miami Beach. Shakira was a big winner at the event. She took home four trophies—for Artist of the Year, Video of the Year (*Suerte*), Best Pop Artist, and Best Female Singer.

Worldwide success thrilled her. She was also excited that MTV was officially recognizing and honoring Latin Americans. Shakira said, "MTV is a worldwide culture and a common place for young people, people who are hungry to be in touch with music from all over the world."

In 2002 Reebok, an athletic shoe company, signed Shakira to a multiyear deal with the company. Though Shakira is in great shape, she doesn't do much formal exercise. Instead, she gets a good workout when she

Shakira performed from the mosh pit at the 2002 MTV Video Music Awards, held at Radio City Music Hall in New York City.

practices and performs her dance routines. Signing Shakira to appear in their ads was unusual. For the first time, Reebok was using an artist instead of an athlete in their commercial ads.

Reebok's marketing department was looking for someone who would appeal to young women. In searching for someone who would move their image beyond rap and hip-hop, they came up with Shakira. In one ad for the company, she crawls, rolls, and belly dances on a sandy beach in her Reebok shoes. She then stomps a peace sign into the sand. A pair of Reebok shoes in her hand transforms into a white dove, symbolizing peace, that flies away. Though the commercial was about athletic shoes, Shakira was also able to share her message of peace.

Shakira announces the Tour of the Mongoose at Rockefeller Center's Rainbow Room in New York City.

Chapter **FOUR**

TOUR OF THE MONGOOSE

IN NOVEMBER **2002,** SHAKIRA EMBARKED ON A SIX-month world tour, the Tour of the Mongoose. Speaking about the tour, she said, "It's a lot of work, but I'm very pleased with what I have. It's more than I ever expected. It's the kind of concert that I've always dreamt about. For 12 years, I've been dreaming to have this show."

Shakira wanted to have every detail of her tour figured out before she took it on the road. She wanted her show to be entertaining and fun—and carry a message. The title of the tour, Shakira explained, is a message about the power of hope to overcome the power of hatred. The mongoose, she said, is "an animal that can defeat the most venomous snake with a bite. . . . We need hope. There's got to be a way to bite the neck of hatred in our lives, the poison in our everyday lives. The world being as it is, we need a mongoose to bite the neck of the snake."

The world tour began in Spain, with many stops in other countries in Europe—then on to Latin America and the United States. "I'm going to give all my creative energy to a loyal public that has witnessed my evolution," Shakira told the press.

When she was starting her tour, she and her band were full of energy and enthusiasm. "We were like teenagers, never tired," said Shakira. "And we didn't have a clue about what was in front of us. We were fresh as carrots."

Onstage, Shakira took on a different persona and musical style for every song. She opened the show by appearing from beneath a giant metal cobra (a poisonous snake) that symbolized hatred. She belly danced, played the drums, and strummed the electric guitar. She tossed her hair and strutted around the stage barefoot.

The concert performance of "Whenever, Wherever" began with a belly-dancing Shakira balancing a lighted candelabra on her head. She ended the song by rising above the stadium-sized crowd in a huge crane. From her sky-high platform, she sang and danced like a circus performer. "She's a freak of nature," says Tim Mitchell, Shakira's lead guitarist, of her enormous onstage confidence and artistic talent.

Not only does Shakira write most of her own material, she is outspoken about her beliefs. During the Tour of the Mongoose, Shakira's songs were accented by messages on an overhead video screen—doves, peace signs, smiley faces, and hearts flashed on the screen, as well as quotes like, "When the power of love overcomes the love of power the world will know peace," by the late rock performer Jimi Hendrix.

While Shakira and her band performed "Octavo Dia" (Eighth Day), two men wearing masks of President George W. Bush and former Iraqi dictator Saddam Hussein appeared on a video screen. They were playing a game of chess. As the video progressed, the viewer saw that the Grim Reaper (death) was controlling the men's movements, as if they were puppets. The image was a reference to the violence and wars in the Middle East and the role that the United States and Iraq were playing in the ongoing conflict.

During the show, Shakira addressed the audience. "Pop stars are not supposed to stick their noses into politics, but I prefer to break the rules," she said while performing at the United Center in Chicago, Illinois. "Why is it so difficult to love one another?" She then did something bold. She asked the people to "take the hand of the person next to you and tell them you love them."

Bridging the differences between cultures—accepting one another's differences—is the only way to world peace, Shakira believes. "I am a pop star, but I also have an opinion," she told *Blender*. "I grew up in a country that has existed under the whip of violence for 40 years, so how can I not? You know, in my country a five-year-old kid knows not only Disney and Mickey Mouse, but also of guerrillas and paramilitaries." She was referring to the rebel troops and small armies involved in the violence surrounding the cocaine trade in Colombia.

Shakira also has a strong opinion about business decisions. She told business manager Freddy DeMann that she wanted the Tour of the Mongoose to make an appearance in Argentina. DeMann thought it was a bad idea. After all, her relationship with Antonio had hurt her reputation in Argentina. But she insisted, and in May 2003, she and her band performed in Buenos Aires. "I wasn't born here," Shakira told the Argentine audience, speaking in Spanish. "However, some have wanted to exile [banish] me. But you can't exile someone who loves a land. I am a little bit yours and you are a little bit mine. That's inevitable."

When she wasn't performing, Shakira was busy planning her next album and writing songs. She worked herself to near exhaustion during the six-month tour. Toward the end, her body ached from performing the strenuous, athletic show night after night. Her arms

Shakira's 2002–2003 world tour included stops in Barcelona, Spain; Cologne, Germany; and London, England (above), as well as several shows in South America.

developed painful tendonitis (inflammation of the tendons) from the wrist and arm movements of belly dancing. A massage therapist continues to help Shakira manage the pain.

"Married to the Mongoose"

Shakira pushed on, determined not to disappoint her fans. Her exhausting work schedule gave her little free time to spend with her boyfriend. Antonio traveled with her and her parents for much of the tour.

"I'm more married to the mongoose than any other man. [Antonio is] very understanding and supportive," Shakira told California's *Orange County Register*. "He's like the greatest support I have, the best help that I have. He helps me with my emotions, to deal with everything."

While traveling on her tour, Shakira sometimes gave ten to twenty interviews a day. The pressures of fame sometimes got to her. "Already everybody is trying to take a piece out of me," she told the *Miami Herald*. "I'm not new at this. I've been at it for 10 years. . . . I know how to preserve Shakira." She turned to her family, her boyfriend, and her religious faith to help her feel grounded and secure.

The Woman behind the Image

In 2003 *Blender* magazine chose Shakira as the Sexiest Woman in Music Today. Shakira was flattered. "If a 25 year old woman tells you she isn't flattered to be chosen as the sexiest woman in music and put on the cover of a magazine like *Blender*, then I'm sorry, but she is lying," she said. "Of course it's flattering. I cannot deny that. And it is something to tell my children. Especially when I am old and covered in cellulite, which will happen one day."

At the 2003 Toy Fair, the Mattel toy company introduced the first three Shakira Barbie dolls. Each doll has a different outfit, reflecting Shakira's unique and changing look.

Some people consider Shakira to be a sex symbol, but she is also a hard worker for humanitarian causes. In 2003 UNICEF recognized this by appointing her to be a goodwill ambassador.

Other serious concerns occupied Shakira in 2003. She began seeing a therapist because of her fear of death.

IDEALS OF BEAUTY

Shakira believes that society's ideals about beauty are damaging to girls and women, including celebrities. "A few years ago, I considered [cosmetic surgery]," she admitted. "Maybe my eyebrows should be higher. Maybe my lips should be bigger. It was making me really bitter. I'd think, 'I'm not gonna look good for my fans!' But [eventually] I said, 'Forget it.' I started accepting myself the way I am and [realized that] I'm not perfect. My fans will like me as long as I keep writing good songs for them. That's the important thing."

A team of makeup artists, hairdressers, and stylists once surrounded Shakira. She remembers, "When I was 23, I used to wear tons of makeup and layers and layers of foundation. Now I

don't wear foundation, not even for my shows." Shakira came to prefer a natural look. She typically wears very little or no makeup. "There's no better makeup than self-confidence," she says.

Posing at Hotel Palace in Madrid, Spain, Shakira shows her casual style and minimal use of makeup. She was in Spain in October 2003 to accept her role as goodwill ambassador of UNICEF.

Shakira considers herself to be thanatophobic (having an extreme fear of death). "Death of relationships, death of feelings, physical death, my death, but especially the death of people I love," she said. "Lately I've been getting over it a little bit, for my own good."

Shakira liked therapy. "It's like a guided trip inside myself. . . . It's helped me grow—though that doesn't mean I'm mature!" she said.

Performing at the 2005 MTV Video Music Awards in Miami, Florida, Shakira used special effects to heat up her songs.

Chapter **FIVE**

ORAL FIXATION

"ACOUSTIC GUITARS ARE FORBIDDEN," SHAKIRA told her bandmates in 2005. "This is one of the rules. It's going to be all synthesizers." The band listened to her. For several months, they used only synthesizers in their rehearsals, while they worked on material for Shakira's next album. But then she changed her mind again.

"I'm sick of synthesizers," Shakira told the band. "I don't wanna see one more synthesizer! Bring all the acoustic guitars you can."

While the instructions might have been confusing to the band, Shakira had a grand vision behind her instructions. She also had sixty new songs, some in Spanish and some in English, all written in the past several months.

"I get lost in my own thoughts and confusions and fantasies about love, and the . . . songs came to me like that," said Shakira. "I don't know why, because none of the songs were premeditated. I was just there to receive them."

Bridging differences between cultures is a recurring theme of Shakira's work. She wanted to create a body of work that reflected this strongly held value. "I had a dream of having this album break barriers of cultural and language frontiers," Shakira told *Rolling Stone.*

The resulting 2005 release, *Fijación Oral, Vol. 1* (Oral Fixation, Vol. 1) combined elements of new-wave electronic keyboards and acoustic guitars, as well as Latin American and Middle Eastern influences. Shakira also planned to put out an English-language version of the album.

"La Tortura" (Torture), the first single from *Fijación Oral, Vol. 1,* was a duet with Spanish singer Alejandro Sanz. The song is about the pain, or torture, of being betrayed by the one you love. "The lyrics came to me like . . . a dialogue between a man and a woman about unfaithfulness and forgiveness and doubt and love and hate and all of those deep emotions in a relationship," said Shakira.

In the video version of the song, Shakira plays the role of an angry woman who has been cheated on. She and Sanz performed the hit single at the MTV Video Music Awards—making "La Tortura" the first Spanish-language song to be performed on the MTV awards show.

Shakira chose to launch the Spanish-language volume of
Fijación Oral *in Bogotá, Colombia.*

A more open attitude toward diversity in the
United States was good news for multicultural
artists such as Shakira. Talking about her performance in Spanish on MTV, Shakira commented,
"That showed me that things are changing,
definitely—in the world—in America—that people

are much more open, that there's a different kind of reception towards music in Spanish."

The title for *Fijación Oral, Vol. 1* was inspired by Shakira's therapy and by psychoanalyst Sigmund Freud's theory of oral fixation, which begins in babyhood. She explains, "I never overcame that initial stage in every life, which is the oral fixation stage. I'm still there. I've always lived through my mouth, like a person in a jail lives through a window. It's my biggest source of pleasure: what I say, what I sing, the kisses I give, the chocolate I eat—which is, a lot."

Shakira doesn't see her oral fixation as a bad thing. "My new resolution is to find pleasure everywhere, no matter how," she said. However, she admits, "I knew it could be a provocative title. But the word oral is very vast, and that's what I like about it. Through our mouths we discover and explore the world. Our mouth is the first source of pleasure, right?"

Fijación Oral, Vol. 1 was well received in the United States and had the best first-week sales yet for a Spanish-language album. Shakira's video *La Tortura* was also a hit. It became the first Spanish-language video regularly shown on MTV.

A reporter from *Time* wrote, explaining the album's success, "The Spanish-language album is a mixed bag of sugary pop and hip-shaking Latin rock. *Fijación Oral* is vastly better than Shakira's English efforts, which have never had the confidence of her singing in her native tongue. You'll have no choice but to get up and dance."

Music reviewers continued to discuss her unusual voice. "Me, I love its size and its tenderness," said *Village Voice* critic Robert Christgau, "and the vibrato haters compare [her voice] to a sheep or Alanis or a bicycle rider on a cobblestone street."

ORAL FIXATION, VOL. 2

Shakira recorded the sequel album to *Fijación Oral, Vol. 1*—titled *Oral Fixation, Vol. 2*—in Miami (where she currently lives), as well as in Vancouver, Canada; Buenos Aires, Argentina; New York; London; and the Bahamas.

"The Spanish album is strictly romantic," she says. "But the English album embraces more social-oriented topics." About making albums in both Spanish and English, Shakira said, "It was like giving birth—with all the contractions and the pain that are involved in the process of delivering, but also [all the] excitement. And instead of one kid, I had twins!"

The first track on the album, "How Do You Do?" is a mix of English, Hebrew, and Arabic lyrics. Shakira also blended in Gregorian chants (Christian music from medieval times) and phrases from the "Our Father," an ancient Christian prayer. Hebrew is the traditional language of Jews and the national language of Israel. Arabic is the language of, among other people, Palestinians and other Arab Muslims, some of whom are in conflict with Israel. By blending elements of these cultures, Shakira expresses her vision of bringing the world together in forgiveness and peace.

Shakira announces the North American leg of her Oral Fixation *Tour at a 2006 press conference in New York.*

Shakira designed her own album covers. On the cover of *Vol. 1,* she wears a modest, lacy slip dress and holds an infant. The imagery looks like that of the Madonna (Mary, the mother of Jesus) in art history. On the cover of *Vol. 2,* Shakira's belly is bare and her chest is covered with a garland of leaves. She is dressed as the biblical character Eve in the Garden of Eden. Like the baby in the cover art, Eve is an innocent and hasn't experienced the world yet. Shakira's cover was a comment on how we all come into the world with innocence. Our essential natures are peaceful, not violent and at war with one another.

Islamic nations in the Middle East (with the exception of Lebanon, her father's homeland) altered the cover art of *Vol. 2*, surprising Shakira. Women are expected to be modest and cover their bodies in some Islamic cultures. Before Shakira's CD was released in most parts of the Middle East, more leaves were added to her bare skin in the album's cover art. So many leaves covered her body that she appeared to be standing behind a bush.

Some Muslims also felt that the lyrics contained messages that questioned their beliefs about religion and God. "How Do You Do?"—a song that poses questions about religion's role in creating suffering in the world—was removed from the album entirely.

"I understand and respect every culture's mentality and different idiosyncrasies," Shakira commented. "I have travelled the world enough to understand that that's the beauty of our cultures. But I didn't count on being covered with leaves. Or that certain governments in certain countries would ban the song. It's a song about peace."

As always, Shakira was vocal about her beliefs. "There's this mentality that artists should remain aside from politics, but I think that music has such an enormous role in people's lives that it could be something besides entertainment."

At the 2006 MTV Video Music Awards, Shakira opened her performance of "Hips Don't Lie" with graceful belly dance moves from India.

Chapter **SIX**

HER HIPS DON'T LIE

SHAKIRA **NOT ONLY USES HER HIPS FOR BELLY** dancing, but she also uses them to feel and express the rhythm and emotion of a song. This feeling inspired her 2006 hit single, "Hips Don't Lie."

Shakira released the song in a unique way. She was the first artist in history to release a song as a cell phone "ring tone" download. At first, "Hips Don't Lie" was available only to cell phone users connected to the Verizon network.

Once released to the general public in May 2006, the single quickly became the most played song in the history of radio. In June 2006, the first full sales week of the album, 267,000 users downloaded the song, setting a new Nielsen Sound Scan record.

SHAKIRA INSPIRES A BELLY DANCING CRAZE

Dance instructors around the world report that more women than ever want to learn belly dancing. They want to learn how to dance like Shakira and other performers such as Jennifer Lopez. Shakira has danced the Middle Eastern style known as belly dancing since she was a small girl. She continues to belly dance in concert and on her videos. Her 2006 hit single, "Hips Don't Lie," especially inspired women all over the globe to learn the dance.

A theater manager coined the term *belly dancing* in 1893 at the Chicago World's Fair, when a troupe of Middle Eastern dancers performed. From the Middle East, the dance was most often performed by women to entertain one another and to celebrate events such as a birth or a wedding. The dance was done for practical reasons too. It develops strong abdominal muscles, which helps women with childbirth.

Shakira believes that every woman can belly dance: "And I think it's very healthy, and I think it kind of puts you in contact with the feminine aspects inside a woman that we need to develop and that I feel proud of." Gia Khalsa, a belly dance performer and teacher from Portland, Oregon, agrees: "It is a dance by women and about the empowerment of women," she said. "It's about the joy and power and fun of being a woman."

In July 2006, Shakira performed "Hips Don't Lie" at the World Cup (international soccer tournament) in Germany. Backed by four hundred other performers, She sang and danced to "Hips Don't Lie"—working the crowd of excited soccer fans into a frenzy.

AWARD WINNER

In 2006 Shakira was honored with many important recording industry awards. In February she won a Grammy Award for Best Latin Rock/Alternative Album (*Fijación Oral, Vol. 1*).

In April she won four Latin Billboard Music Awards—shared with Spanish singer Alejandro Sanz—for their duet, "La Tortura." Shakira also won the Spirit of Hope Award for her humanitarian work through her Fundación Pies Descalzos. The yearly program gives the award to one person considered exceptional in helping the human race.

The *Hips Don't Lie* video received an MTV Video Music Award for Best Choreography in September. Shakira was also a big winner in November at the 2006 Latin Grammy Awards. The twenty-nine-year-old won five awards—Best Engineered Album for *Fijación Oral, Vol. 1;* Best Female Pop Vocal Album for *Fijación Oral, Vol. 1;* Song of the Year for "La Tortura"; Album of the Year for *Fijación Oral, Vol. 1;* and Record of the Year for "La Tortura."

After picking up her fourth award, Shakira, dressed in a flowing black dress by designer Roberto Cavalli, addressed the audience. "I love you all. . . . You have made me very happy tonight," she said, adding "Everything I know I learned in one place—I want to thank my people, Barranquilla, Colombia."

In her acceptance speech, Shakira also paid tribute to "all Latinos, especially the immigrants here in the

During her visit to Barranquilla, Shakira taught belly dance moves to children at a neighborhood school.

United States who are just trying to achieve their dream—that someday they receive the recognition that they deserve."

HEART OF GOLD

In July 2006, Shakira worked with Hard Rock International to help children who are victims of violence in Colombia. She donated several stage costumes from her 2005 world tour, as well as the dress she wore on the cover of *Oral Fixation,* to Hard Rock Café's memorabilia collection. The costumes are on display in Hard Rock Cafés worldwide. In thanks, Hard Rock International donated $80,000 to the Pies Descalzos foundation.

In November Shakira traveled to San Salvador, the capital of the Central American country of El Salvador. She was taking part in the "Make the Difference by Not Being Indifferent" campaign. When Shakira is on tour, she is often too busy to keep up with TV news and current events. "But I do get a chance to look into a child's eyes," she says, "and speak with the local people and understand what they are going through."

A bloody civil war had ravaged El Salvador from 1980 to 1992. It left an aftermath of poverty and gang violence. In the capital city, Shakira spoke to a crowd of eight thousand children and teens. Coming from war-torn Colombia, she had a deep understanding of the situation. "I come from a difficult country, and thus, know and understand what happens to Salvadorean youth, because many believe there is no better future and choose unlawfulness and violence, feeling it is the only way," said Shakira.

A hope-filled message ended her speech. "We only have one life to live," the singer said. "Let's live with dignity. And I invite you, starting today, to make a difference."

ALAS

In December 2006, Shakira joined forces with author and friend Gabriel García Márquez to launch a foundation, the Association for Latin American Solidarity (ALAS). The organization to fight poverty in Latin America is based in the Central American country of Panama. ALAS raises money for impoverished Latin American children and teenagers.

The organization's opening event was similar to the 1985 Live Aid concert, which was a multivenue, live rock-concert benefit for victims of famine in Ethiopia. An estimated 1.5 billion television viewers worldwide watched the live, satellite-linked broadcast. ALAS's event focused on efforts to help people in Latin America. Many musical artists offered to perform for the organization, including Ricky Martin, Alejandro Sanz, Miguel Bosé, and Daniela Mercury. Shakira said, "We want this to be an event that brings world attention to poverty in Latin America, which is virtually invisible to the rest of the world."

Shakira launched the ALAS foundation in Panama City, Panama. The word alas means "wings" in Spanish, so the foundation chose a logo showing Latin and South America outlined by a pair of wings.

FUNDACIÓN PIES DESCALZOS

hakira's homeland is a beautiful country, with a tropical climate and ocean beaches. But Colombia has been the victim of civil unrest and violence for decades. As a result, almost three million people are poverty-stricken or homeless. Nearly eight hundred thousand children are the victims of violence or displacement.

About two million children in Colombia can't go to school. "Each of them has a name, a heart, a dream and their lives are as valuable as yours and mine," says Shakira. In 1998 she took her own money and founded Fundación Pies Descalzos (Bare Feet Foundation) to help build schools for the children of Colombia.

The first school was built in 2003. The foundation has hired twenty-four teachers. Since then, the organization has built several more schools. Because of the new schools, more than fifteen hundred children receive meals and schooling.

Shakira has learned that people working together for a common goal can move mountains. "At one point, I realized that an artist alone can't do it," said Shakira. "You need a serious, efficient, organized, honest team. What you want to immediately do and what you can actually do are two different things. But I have also learned that you can accomplish what you imagine." She hopes that her foundation will continue to grow, possibly expanding to developing countries around the world.

On April 3, 2006, the United Nations honored Shakira in a ceremony for her work with the Pies Descalzos foundation. At the event, Shakira said, "Let's not forget that at the end of this day when we all go home, 960 children will have died in Latin America."

HISPANIC OF THE YEAR

Shakira received a great honor in 2006. *Hispanic* magazine named her Hispanic of the Year, in honor of her accomplishments in the music business as well as her work on behalf of Colombia's victims of violence. "I do feel a huge satisfaction seeing all the progress [made by the foundation], and the betterment of children, but I am also troubled knowing how much more there is to do," Shakira told *Hispanic*. "I am constantly thinking about the next steps, because these kids deserve our hard work to provide them with education. That is the key to their future."

At every concert and when she wins an award, Shakira typically thanks her homeland, Colombia. "People know and love me all over the world. But ultimately, I dedicate my work to my country, Colombia," she says. "They need reasons to smile and reasons to celebrate. They need good news."

"AN ENORMOUSLY APPEALING SPRITE"

Near the end of 2006, Shakira set off on her second world tour, the *Oral Fixation* Tour. In the show, she showcased her hit songs from both volumes of her recent CD, as well as her recent smash single, "Hips Don't Lie." Some reporters commented on the star's warm, down-to-earth personality. "For 'Whenever, Wherever,' she skipped into the crowd and spent a long time chanting, clapping, hugging and urging people around her to sing and clap with her, startling in a show like this and for a star of her stature," said Jordan Levin in the *Miami Herald*.

The tour showcased Shakira's eclectic musical style. She belly danced, played the harmonica, and during "Don't Bother," she played an electric guitar encrusted with sparkly, pink crystals.

The *Miami Herald* reported that "No" was "a beautiful song gone poisonously painful." The *Herald* said that Shakira, wearing a flowing red gown, "used long sticks to swirl enormous red fabric wings into the air like a giant, diaphanous butterfly, as if the emotion in the song was spiraling out of her heart and into the air."

After the *Oral Fixation* Tour passed through San Jose, California, the *San Francisco Chronicle* reported that Shakira was "an enormously appealing sprite." She was "so tiny it's as if she were built on three-quarter scale."

Chicago Tribune reporter Greg Kot observed that Shakira's show was "low-tech," compared to the shows of performers such as Christina Aguilera and Madonna. "But unlike those pop queens, Shakira radiated a joy in performing."

Shakira loves her work—and it shows. "I get to build bridges that bring me closer to people," she says. She adds, "Just having the freedom of expressing myself and creating; it is a beautiful thing."

Shakira's 2006 Latin Grammy Awards performance featured an intense acoustic rendition of "La Pared" (The Wall).

Chapter **SEVEN**

CAPTAIN OF HER OWN SHIP

A MUSICIAN WHO ACCOMPLISHES EVERYTHING THAT
Shakira does has to work hard. And Shakira is hard-
working. While rehearsing, her mind is often racing
with other thoughts about production, such as light-
ing, sound, and video. Sometimes she feels as if her
mind will burst from all the details in her head. Her
unique vision leads her to make many of her own
business decisions and to take part in even the tiniest
parts of her career.

Shakira doesn't want to stop being a perfectionist.
"Why does something have to be wrong when it can
be right?" she pondered in Spanish on her DVD doc-
umentary, *Shakira: Live and Off the Record.* "Why
does something have to be right when it can be

great? Why does something have to be great when it can be magnificent?"

She also expects the people around her to work just as hard as she does. She prefers to work with her friends, the people she has known a long time and trusts. Her longtime lead guitarist, Tim Mitchell, cowrote "Whenever, Wherever" with her. At first he didn't understand her creative process. For example, when Mitchell listens to music, he *hears* it with his ears. But when Shakira listens to music, she *feels* it with her body. "She'd tell me, 'I don't feel this music in my hips,' Now we work on something and I'm like, 'Why don't you ask your hips what they think?'" Mitchell joked.

While she works closely with others, the creative star believes that only she can carry out many of the details of her unique vision. "I like to be the captain of my own ship," says Shakira.

"THE WOMAN IS THE NECK"

Petite and feminine, Shakira takes an aggressive approach when she's making important business deals. She's learned many things over the course of her career. For example, she no longer makes impulsive business decisions. "I've learned to say those magic words: 'Let me think about it.' That gives you time to digest information and make smart decisions."

Shakira keeps much control over both the creative and the business aspects of her career. But she still has to cooperate with other musicians, producers, directors, and businesspeople. Many of the people she works with are men. "[Men] don't like a woman telling them what to do, no matter how famous you are," Shakira observed. "Even the guys who love their mother."

Working with the businesspeople in the music industry challenges her. "We see our careers in the long term and they see them in the short term," she said. "We're different. But we need each other. It's like Batman needs the Joker—something like that."

Shakira has discovered how she works best with men. "You have to let them believe that they came up with the idea," she laughed. "I love, in [the movie] *My Big Fat Greek Wedding,* when the mother says to the daughter that the man is the head of the household but the woman is the neck, and she can turn the head whenever she wants to."

DREAMS AND DAYDREAMS

Though she is famous, Shakira doesn't care about hanging out with other famous people or wearing designer clothing. And even though she is very wealthy, she hates to shop. "I'm probably one of the few girls in the world who can say that," she said. "But it's such a burden—trying stuff on, taking stuff off, making decisions. It's exhausting."

Spending her free time jamming with her band, jotting down song ideas, or just hanging out with Antonio and her family are priorities for Shakira. She has

German artist Dieter Patt unveiled a 16-foot metal sculpture of Shakira in Barranquilla, Colombia, in March 2006. The following November, children gathered around it before Shakira's Oral Fixation show.

written the lyrics and music to dozens of songs. She is always grateful when a new song comes to her. "I feel that inspiration inside of me is a gift that the gods send me. They send me the opportunity to create," she said. "So, every time I write a song, I celebrate it as if it were a miracle."

Though she is dedicated to her musical career, she daydreams about having children with Antonio, but not yet. She sees being a parent as a serious job—the biggest project she'll ever undertake—and she wants to be ready. "I just have to do a couple more things before I become a committed mother," says Shakira.

She'd also like to have a big farm someday with horses and a vegetable garden. "There are so many dreams that I still hold inside, that I think this life is not going to be enough for me to accomplish them all," she says.

Shakira sometimes has to remind herself to just enjoy her life and all that she has accomplished. "Because, you know, we always go through the present blindfolded with our hearts in the past and our minds in the future," Shakira says. "And that way we never enjoy the here and now."

"SHAKIRA TROUBLE DRAMA"

Stars don't stay on top all their lives, as Shakira knows very well. "One day you're here and you're desirable for people, but that's not going to last forever," she said. "Everything has its own time, and at some point I know I'm going to fall as well. I just wonder how painful it's going to be when I touch the floor."

While being famous can be challenging, Shakira finds that being an artist is challenging too. She sees her creative labors as being like the labor of childbirth. "Every day, I suffer over decisions," she says. "People around me see me cry and see me very insecure. I guess I don't feel like I'm delivering a baby if I don't feel the pain and the contractions, you know?"

Fortunately, Shakira's partner in life is patient with her ups and downs. "Antonio's a saint, believe me," says Shakira. "I'm a drama queen. Drama is my last name. Trouble's my middle name, and Drama is my last name. Shakira Trouble Drama."

RARE SPARE TIME

Reading is one of the things Shakira likes to do. "I love history, and I wish I knew more about it," she told *Rolling Stone*. "I started my career very early—right out of high school—and I couldn't go to a university because I already had a contract. It has been only music since I was thirteen years old. So there's always a part of me that's hungry."

Shakira likes the Harry Potter movies. "I have a narrow range of movies I can see," she says. "I resist watching terror, horror, action movies. I limit the kind of stuff I want to put in my brain. On TV, I only watch Cartoon Network and Animal Planet."

When she's not performing, Shakira prefers comfortable jeans and sweatshirts. Her favorite sweatshirt is a black zippered sweatshirt with stripes on the sleeves. Antonio prefers Shakira to have a natural look. "He would be the happiest man on earth if I was in sneakers and a rock and roll T-shirt," she said. "He doesn't like when I get made up."

Antonio sometimes gives Shakira advice about clothing. "My boyfriend, he has a good eye," Shakira told *Flare*. "He's not a stylist, but I wish I listened to him

Shakira and her tour crew visit the Great Pyramids of Giza in Egypt in March 2007. The Oral Fixation Tour *took Shakira around the world, with concerts in Egypt, India, and the United Arab Emirates.*

more in the past when he told me 'Don't wear that.' When I see pictures of myself in [some] outfits, I think, 'Oh my God, he was right.'"

A small scar marks the middle of Shakira's forehead. She got the scar when she had smallpox as a young girl. "It's lucky I got it on my third eye," said Shakira, referring to the spot that in some cultures represents psychic ability. "My intuition powers have definitely developed since then."

Shakira loves to eat, especially traditional Colombian food. "Colombian food is really good—and really fattening," she points out. She likes traditional Colombian dishes such as *sancocho* (a soup served with rice), *corozos* (a sweet-and-sour Colombian fruit), and fried yucca (a root) that tastes like french fries. She also likes Colombian coffee, but she usually limits herself to one cup a day. And she loves chocolate. "I like any kind of chocolate," says Shakira. "American, Belgian, Swiss—I don't discriminate."

No matter how busy her schedule is, Shakira always takes time for a two-hour lunch, at least. Like many Colombians, mealtime for her is for relaxing, sharing thoughts, and savoring food and drink with friends and family. She adds, "I really enjoy eating. If it could be a hobby, it would be mine."

The Catholic faith remains important to Shakira. She attends Catholic Mass and prays regularly. "Poor God, I must be driving him crazy with the big list of things that I'm always asking for," says Shakira. "But my God is very friendly and is always there waiting for me to call him to give me a hand."

"CITIZEN OF THE WORLD"

Songwriting and singing are Shakira's lifetime passions. But she plans to do more acting in the future, including starring in a film called *Dare to Love Me*. Renowned Mexican American actor-director Alfonso Arau is the director. The film, to be shot in Romania, is set in 1930s Paris, France. Shakira plays the love interest of Argentine tango legend Carlos Gardel.

Shakira creates waves of color with one of her favorite props, a pair of sticks that trail yards of flowing fabric. This performance took place at the Great Pyramids of Giza in Egypt.

When Shakira is on tour, her parents come with her. She considers her parents to be her best friends. "I live on the plane most of the time," said Shakira. "I'm always on the road. My family travels with me all the time. They are what I consider home."

With her "home"—her family and the man she loves—Shakira will continue to travel the world to share her music and promote humanitarian causes. "The world's shrunk," she says. "The planet was never smaller, no? I do feel global. I feel like a citizen of the world."

MAJOR INTERNATIONAL AWARDS

2007

PEOPLE'S CHOICE AWARD
Favorite Pop Song–"Hips Don't Lie"

2006

ALMA AWARDS
Outstanding Female
Musical Performer
Best Spanish Album
Fijación Oral, Vol. 1

AMERICAN MUSIC AWARDS
Favorite Latin Artist

GRAMMY AWARDS
Best Latin Rock/Alternative
Album–*Fijación Oral Vol. 1*

LATIN BILLBOARD MUSIC AWARDS
Hot Latin Song of the Year–
"La Tortura"
Hot Latin Song of the Year, Vocal
Duo of the Year–"La Tortura"
Female Latin Pop Album of the
Year–*Fijación Oral Vol. 1*
Latin Pop Airplay Song of the Year,
Duo or Group–"La Tortura"
Latin Ringtone of the Year–
"La Tortura"
Spirit of Hope Award

LATIN GRAMMY AWARDS
Record of the Year–"La Tortura"
Album of the Year–
Fijación Oral Vol. 1
Song of the Year–"La Tortura"
Best Female Pop Vocal
Album–*Fijación Oral, Vol. 1*
Best Engineered Album–
Fijación Oral, Vol. 1

LATIN MUSIC AWARDS
Pop Album of the Year–
Fijación Oral Vol. 1
Best Pop Group or Duo–
"La Tortura"
Pop Song of the Year–"La Tortura"

MTV VIDEO MUSIC AWARDS
Best Choreography–"Hips Don't Lie"
Song of the Year–"Hips Don't Lie"

NRJ MUSIC AWARDS
Best International Song–"La Tortura"

WORLD MUSIC AWARDS
Best-Selling Latin Artist

2005

AMERICAN MUSIC AWARDS
Favorite Latin Artist

MTV EUROPE MUSIC AWARDS
Best Female Artist

MTV LATIN AMERICAN VIDEO MUSIC AWARDS
Video of the Year–*La Tortura*

Artist of the Year
Best Female Artist
Best Pop Artist
Best Artist—Central

WORLD MUSIC AWARDS
Best-Selling Latin Artist

2004

PREMIO LO NUESTRO
Best Female Pop Artist

2003

AMADEUS AWARD
Best Song of the Year–
"Whenever, Wherever"

BMI AWARD
Latin Song of the Year–"Suerte"

ECHO AWARD
Best Female Artist

LUNA AWARD
Best Latin Pop Artist

NRJ MUSIC AWARDS
Best International Song–
"Whenever, Wherever"
Best International Album–
Laundry Service
Best International Female Artist

WORLD MUSIC AWARD
Best Latin Female Artist

2002

LATIN GRAMMY AWARDS
Best Music Video–*Suerte*

**MTV LATIN AMERICAN VIDEO
MUSIC AWARDS**
Video of the Year–*Suerte*
Artist of the Year
Best Female Singer
Best Pop Artist

MUCH MUSIC CANADA AWARDS
Best International Video–
Whenever, Wherever
Best International Artist

PREMIO LO NUESTRO
Best Female Pop Artist

PREMIOS OYE!
Album of the Year (International)–
Laundry Service
Album of the Year (National)–
Servicio de Lavandería

RITMO LATINO MUSIC AWARD
Best Video–*Whenever, Wherever*

TMF AWARD
Best New Artist International

2001

LATIN BILLBOARD MUSIC AWARD
Best Latin Album–*MTV Unplugged*

GLOBO AWARD
Best Female Pop Album

GRAMMY AWARD
Best Latin Pop Album–
MTV Unplugged

PREMIO LO NUESTRO
Rock Album of the Year–
MTV Unplugged
Rock Performance of the Year

2000

LATIN GRAMMY AWARDS
Best Female Pop Vocal
Performance–"Ojos Asi"
Best Female Rock Vocal
Performance–"Octavo Dia"

**MTV LATIN AMERICAN VIDEO
MUSIC AWARDS**
People's Choice Award–Favorite
Video–*Ojos Así*

1999

BILLBOARD LATIN MUSIC AWARDS
Best Female Pop Artist

CASANDRA AWARD
Best Album of the Year

PREMIO AMIGO
Best Latin American Solo Artist

PREMIO LO NUESTRO
Best Pop Artist, Female

TV Y NOVELAS MAGAZINE
Colombian Artist of the Century

1998

WORLD MUSIC AWARD
Best Latin Artist

1997

BILLBOARD LATIN MUSIC AWARDS
Best Album–*Pies Descalzos*
Best Video–*Estoy Aquí*
Best New Artist

CASANDRA AWARD
Best Latin Female Singer

PREMIO LO NUESTRO
Best Female Pop Artist
Best New Artist

1994

TV Y NOVELAS [MAGAZINE] AWARDS
Best National Artist

SHAKIRA'S MAJOR RELEASES

1991: *Magia*
1993: *Peligro*
1996: *Pies Descalzos*
1998: *¿Dónde Están Los Ladrones?*
2000: *MTV Unplugged*
2001: *Laundry Service/Servicio de Lavandería*
2004: *Live & Off the Record*
2005: *Fijación Oral, Vol. 1*
2005: *Oral Fixation, Vol. 2*
2007: *Oral Fixation Tour: Live from Miami*

TIMELINE

1977 Shakira Isabel Mebarak Ripoll is born on February 2, 1977, in Barranquilla, Colombia.

1985 At eight Shakira writes her first song.

1990 Shakira, thirteen, signs her first recording contract with Sony Music Latin America.

1991 Shakira's first album, *Magia* (Magic), is released.

1993 *Peligro* (Danger), Shakira's second album, comes out.

1994 At seventeen Shakira moves to Bogotá, Colombia, with her mother.

1996 She joins the cast of the Colombian telenovela *El Oasis* (The Oasis).

Shakira's third album and first international release comes out. *Pies Descalzos* (Bare Feet) becomes a number-one hit in eight countries and goes platinum in the United States.

1997 Shakira leaves her job as an actress on the soap opera *El Oasis* and moves to the United States.

1998 She forms the Fundación Pies Descalzos (Bare Feet Foundation) to help the impoverished children of Colombia.

Emilio Estefan, singer Gloria Estefan's husband, becomes Shakira's manager and producer. Shakira's fourth album, *¿Dónde Están los Ladrones?* (Where Are the Thieves?), is released.

2000 Shakira meets her boyfriend, Antonio de la Rúa.

At the very first Latin Grammy Awards, Shakira wins the award for the Best Female Pop Vocal ("Ojos Así" [Eyes Like Yours]) and Best Female Rock Vocal ("Octavo Dia" [Eighth Day]).

Shakira's live album *MTV Unplugged* is released.

2001 Shakira dyes her hair blonde.

Shakira's first mostly English-language album, *Laundry Service*, is a huge hit. More than 13 million copies of the album sell worldwide.

Antonio de la Rúa proposes to Shakira in Rome.

2002 Shakira embarks on a six-month world tour, the Tour of the Mongoose.

2003 Shakira is named a goodwill ambassador for the humanitarian organization UNICEF (United Nations International Children's Emergency Fund)—becoming the youngest person to be placed in the position.

2004 *Live and Off the Record* (En Vivo Y En Privado), a DVD and a ten-song CD from her 2002–2003 world tour, Tour of the Mongoose, is released.

2005 Shakira releases an album in both Spanish and English, *Fijación Oral, Vol. 1* and *Oral Fixation, Vol. 2*.

2006 Shakira releases her single, "Hips Don't Lie." The song becomes the most played song on the radio in history.

2007 Shakira's concert album, *Oral Fixation Tour: Live from Miami*, is released.

Shakira appears on the Grammy Awards and performs "Hips Don't Lie" with Wyclef Jean.

SOURCE NOTES

7   Jim Abbott, "High-Spirited Shakira's Hips, Voice Don't Lie," *Orlando Sentinel*, September 16, 2006.

8   J. Freedom du Lac, "In Any Language, a Whole Lotta Shakira Goin' On," *Washington Post*, August 31, 2006.

8   Chuck Arnold and Linda Trischitta, "Bomba Shell," *People*, February 11, 2002, 134.

8   Rosie Amorose, e-mail message and telephone conversation with author, February 3, 2007.

8   Arnold and Trischitta, "Bomba Shell."

9   Shakira, interviewed by Chris Connelly, "Hips, Lies and Hot Videotape," *ABCnews.go.com*, March 27, 2006, http://abcnews.go.com/2020/print?id=1772538 (January 11, 2007).

10 Scott Athorne, "South American Dream," *Sunday Times* (London), January 15, 2006.

10 Erik Hedegaard, "The Shakira Complex," *New Yorker*, September 26, 2005, 46-47.

10 Rob Tannenbaum, "Miss Universe," *Blender*, July 2005, http://www.blender.com/guide/articles.aspx?id=1679 (January 21, 2007).

10 Ibid.

11 Chris Willman, "Shakira," *Entertainment Weekly*, September 15, 2006, 76.

11 Christopher John Farley, "The Making of a Rocker," *Time* (Australia), December 17, 2001, 70.

12 Nick Duerden, "The Sexiest Woman in Music Today: Shakira," *Blender*, March 2003, http://www.blender.com/guide/articles.aspx?id=121 (January 21, 2007).

12 Athorne, "South American Dream."

12 Duerden, "The Sexiest Woman."

13 Athorne, "South American Dream."

13 Duerden, "The Sexiest Woman."

16 Tannenbaum, "Miss Universe."

18 Vh1.com, "Driven: Shakira; About the Episode," *vh1.com*, November 10, 2005, http://www.vh1.com/shows/dyn/driven/96614/episode_about.jhtml (January 21, 2007).

18 Ted Kessler, "Colombian Gold," *Observer* (London), July 14, 2002.

18 Athorne, "South American Dream."

19 Kessler, "Colombian Gold."

19 Ibid.

19 Evan Wright, "Shakira," *Rolling Stone,* April 11, 2002, 68.

20 Kessler, "Colombian Gold."

20 Vh1.com, "Driven: Shakira."

20 Ibid.

21 Mim Udovitch, "Shakira," *Rolling Stone,* February 14, 2002, 30.

21 Zena Burns, "It's Not My Hobby to Show My Belly," *Teen People,* May 2006, 8.

23 Udovitch, "Shakira."

23 Kessler, "Colombian Gold."

24 Athorne, "South American Dream."

24 Tannenbaum, "Miss Universe."

24 Ibid.

25 Ibid.

25 Ibid.

25 Ibid.

26 Mim Udovitch, "Shakira," *Rolling Stone,* October 31, 2002, 102.

26 Ibid.

26 Ibid.

27 Wright, "Shakira."

27 Kessler, "Colombian Gold."

30 Athorne, "South American Dream."

30 Udovitch, October 31, 2002.

31 Kessler, "Colombian Gold."

31 Udovitch, February 14, 2002.

34 Vh1.com, "Driven: Shakira."

36 Mim Udovitch, "Shakira: She's Blonde, She's Beautiful, but She's Not Another Britney," *Teen People,* Summer 2002, Music Supplement, 34.

39 Rob Patterson, "Shakira Shakes Up the Contemporary Music Scene," *BMI.com,* March 23, 2006, http://www.bmi.com/ musicworld/entry/533099 (January 9, 2007).

40 Barry Rust, "Shakira," *Scholastic Action,* September 17, 2002, 6.

41 Lydia Martin, "Latin Superstar Shakira Hopes to Clean Up with 'Laundry Service,'" *Miami Herald,* November 21, 2001.

41 Barry Rust, "Shakira," *Scholastic Action,* September 17, 2002, 6.

41 Martin, "Latin Superstar."

41 Rust, "Shakira."

43 Martin, "Latin Superstar."

44 Ibid.

44 Ibid.

45 Ibid.

45 Kessler, "Colombian Gold."

45 Ibid.

46 Udovitch, "Shakira: She's Blonde."

46 Kessler, "Colombian Gold."

46 Udovitch, "Shakira: She's Blonde."

46 Ibid.

47 Ibid.

47 Ibid.

49 Ericka Souter, "Chatter," *People,* March 11, 2002, 156.

49 Cara Lynn Shultz, "Shakir Attack," *Teen People,* March 2002, 87.

49 Leila Cobo, "Epic's Shakira 'Serves' a Bilingual Album," *Billboard,* November 10, 2001, 5.

49 Teresa Puente, "Blond Thing a Bombshell for Latinas," *Chicago Tribune,* March 15, 2002.

50 Jennifer L. Peters, "Feeling Their Roots: Are Female Stars Hiding Their Ethnic Roots?" *Know Your World Extra,* November 29, 2002, 4.

51 Richard Chang, "Latin Pop Star Is More Than Blonde Curls and Head-Turning Outfits," *Orange County Register,* November 14, 2002.

51 Cobo, "Epic's Shakira."

51 Shultz, "Shakir Attack."

52 Chang, "Latin Pop Star."

52 Kessler, "Colombian Gold."

53 Ibid.

53 Thor Christensen, Mario Tarradell, and Rob Clark, "Reviews of Releases by Garth Brooks, Natalie Merchant, Shakira" *Dallas Morning News,* November 13, 2001.

53   "Rock 'N' Rumba," *Flare,* April 2006, 74.

54   Udovitch, "Shakira: She's Blonde."

56   Bob Port, "Shakira Blasts Labor Abuses," *New York Daily News,* April 30, 2002.

56   Ibid.

56   Ibid.

56   Leila Cobo, "Shakira Wins 5 MTV Latin Awards," *Billboard,* November 2, 2002, 3.

59   Chang, "Latin Pop Star."

60   ABC News, "Shakira to Begin World Tour in Spain," *ABCNews.go.com,* March 23, 2006, http://abcnews.go.com/ Entertainment/print?id=1759781 (January 11, 2007).

60   Shakira, *Shakira: Live and Off the Record,* DVD, directed by Ramiro Agulla and Esteban Sapir (Sony Music Entertainment, 2004).

60   "Shakira."

61   *Shakira: Live and Off the Record.*

61   Laura Emerick, "Not Difficult at All to Love Shakira," *Chicago Sun-Times,* January 20, 2003.

61   Ibid.

62   Duerden, "The Sexiest Woman."

62   *Shakira: Live and Off the Record.*

64   Chang, "Latin Pop Star."

64   Martin, "Latin Superstar."

64   Duerden, "The Sexiest Woman."

66   Burns, "It's Not My Hobby."

66   "Rock 'N' Rumba."

66   Burns, "It's Not My Hobby."

67   Udovitch, February 14, 2002.

67   Tannenbaum, "Miss Universe."

69   Ibid.

69   Ibid.

70   Jordan Levin, "Colombian Singing Star Shakira Offers New Take on Life and Love," *Miami Herald,* June 3, 2005.

70   Lauren Gitlin, "Viva Shakira," *Rolling Stone,* August 25, 2005, 12.

70   Levin, "Colombian Singing Star."

72   MTV, "First Ladies: Shakira," [video clip/short interview on website], *MTV.com,* n.d., http://www.mtv.com/music/artist/

shakira/artist.jhtml#/music/artist/shakira/videos.jhtml
(January 20, 2007).

72 Tannenbaum, "Miss Universe."

72 Ibid.

72 Ibid.

72 Carolina A. Miranda, "6 Sizzling CDs from South of the
Border," *Time,* October 16, 2006, 83.

73 Robert Christgau, "A Hot Little Weirdo," *Village Voice,*
January 13, 2006.

73 Lauren Gitlin and Andy Greene, Brian Hiatt, Kevin
O'Donnell, Austin Scaggs, and Gillian Telling, "Shakira:
Oral Fixation, Vol. 2," *Rolling Stone,* October 20, 2005, 26.

73 "Rock 'N' Rumba."

75 Victoria Segal, "Forbidden Fruit," *Times* (London), February
11, 2006.

75 Ibid.

78 Udovitch, February 14, 2002.

78 Maryellen Fillo, "Belly Dancing Hip Again," *Hartford
Courant,* June 6, 2006.

79 Robert Dominguez, Maite Junco, and Leo Standora.
"Shakira Crowned New Latin Queen: Sexy Singer Wins 4
Grammys, *New York Daily News,* November 3, 2006.

79 Jordan Levin, "Shakira, Calle 13 Dominate Awards, but
Show Falls Flat: In a Show That Lacked Sizzle, Shakira
Was the Standout Winner at This Year's Latin Grammy
Awards," *Miami Herald,* November 3, 2006.

80 Ibid.

81 Mark Holston, "Side B," *Hispanic,* December 2006–January
2007, 68–72.

81 Sabine Dolan, "Shakira, UNICEF Launch Campaign for
Peace in El Salvador," *unicef.org,* November 6, 2006,
http://www.unicef.org/videoaudio/ramfiles/6686h-
elsalvadorshakira.ram (January 10, 2007).

81 Ibid.

82 Leila Cobo, "Shakira Plans Live (Latin) Aid," *Billboard,* April
22, 2006, 58–59.

83 Shakira, "My Story," *Shakira.com,* http://www.shakira.com
(January 9, 2007) [n.d.]

83 Leila Cobo, "Dreams Come True," *Billboard,* April 29, 2006,
12.

83 Aaron Parsley, "Shakira Honored at United Nations," *Teen People*, April 4, 2006.

84 Holston, "Side B."

84 Duerden, "The Sexiest Woman."

84 Jordan Levin, "Second Time Around, Shakira a True Superstar," *Miami Herald*, September 16, 2006.

85 Ibid.

85 Joel Selvin, "Along Her Path to World Domination, Shakira Conquers San Jose," *San Francisco Chronicle*, August 21, 2006.

85 Greg Kot, "Shakira Shows She's More Than 'Hips' and a Belly Button," *Chicago Tribune*, August 28, 2006.

85 Shakira, "My Story," Shakira.com, http://www.shakira.com (January 9, 2007).

88 *Shakira: Live and Off the Record.*

88 Shakira, interviewed by Chris Connelly.

88 Burns, "It's Not My Hobby."

89 Ibid.

89 *Shakira: Live and Off the Record.*

89 Burns, "It's Not My Hobby."

89 Hedegaard, "The Shakira Complex."

90 Mario Tarradell, "For Colombian Star Shakira, Superstardom Is Her Destiny," *Dallas Morning News*, December 12, 2001.

91 Levin, "Colombian Singing Star."

91 MTV, "First Ladies: Shakira."

91 Udovitch, February 14, 2002.

91 Athorne, "South American Dream."

91 Tannenbaum, "Miss Universe."

92 Ibid.

92 Lindsay Goldenberg, "Shakira," *Rolling Stone*, January 13, 2002, 26.

92 *Chicago Sun-Times*, "The Lady Is a Champ," January 17, 2003.

92 "Rock 'N' Rumba."

93 Ibid.

93 Athorne, "South American Dream."

94 Simon Perry, "Oral History," *People Weekly*, December 19, 2005, 93–94.

94   Ibid.
94   *People*, "The 50 Most Beautiful People 2002: Shakira," May 13, 2002, 150.
94   Udovitch, "Shakira: She's Blonde."
95   Chang, "Latin Pop Star."
95   Tannenbaum, "Miss Universe."

SELECTED BIBLIOGRAPHY

Burns, Zena. "It's Not My Hobby to Show My Belly." *Teen People*, May 2006, 8.

Cobo, Leila. "'Dreams Come True.'" *Billboard*, April 29, 2006, 12.

Hedegaard, Erik. "The Shakira Complex." *New Yorker*, September 26, 2005, 46–47.

Holston, Mark. "Side B." *Hispanic*, December 2006–January 2007, 68–72.

Levin, Jordan. "Colombian Singing Star Shakira Offers New Take on Life and Love." *Miami Herald*, June 3, 2005.

Perry, Simon. "Oral History." *People Weekly*, December 19, 2005, 93–94.

Rust, Barry. "Shakira." *Scholastic Action*, September 17, 2002, 6–7.

Segal, Victoria. "Forbidden Fruit." *Times* (London), February 11, 2006.

FURTHER READING AND WEBSITES

Benson, Michael. *Gloria Estefan.* Minneapolis: Twenty-First Century Books, 2000.

Day, Holly. *Shakira.* San Diego: Lucent Books, 2007.

Márquez, Héron. *Latin Sensations.* Minneapolis: Twenty-First Century Books, 2001.

Pies Descalzos Foundation
http://www.fundacionpiesdescalzos.com/english/index.php
Read about what Shakira's foundation does to help children in Colombia.

Rivera, Ursula. *Shakira.* Danbury, CT: Children's Press, 2003.

Shakira's Official Website
http://shakira.com
Get news about Shakira, check her concert dates, and watch her music videos at her official website.

Streissguth, Thomas. *Colombia in Pictures.* Minneapolis: Twenty-First Century Books, 2004.

WEBSITES

INDEX

OTHER TITLES FROM TWENTY-FIRST CENTURY BOOKS AND BIOGRAPHY®:

Ariel Sharon
Arnold Schwarzenegger
Benito Mussolini
Benjamin Franklin
Bill Gates
Billy Graham
Carl Sagan
Che Guevara
Chief Crazy Horse
Colin Powell
Coretta Scott King
Daring Pirate Women
Edgar Allan Poe
Eleanor Roosevelt
Fidel Castro
Frank Gehry
George Lucas
George W. Bush
Gloria Estefan
Gwen Stefani
Hillary Rodham Clinton
Jack Kerouac
Jacques Cousteau
Jane Austen
J.K. Rowling
Joseph Stalin
Latin Sensations
Legends of Dracula
Legends of Santa Claus
Malcolm X

Mao Zedong
Mark Twain
Martha Stewart
Maya Angelou
Napoleon Bonaparte
Nelson Mandela
Osama bin Laden
Pope Benedict XVI
Pope John Paul II
Queen Cleopatra
Queen Elizabeth I
Queen Latifah
Rosie O'Donnell
Russell Simmons
Saddam Hussein
Shakira
Stephen Hawking
The Beatles
Thurgood Marshall
Tiger Woods
Tony Blair
Vera Wang
V.I. Lenin
Vladimir Putin
Wilma Rudolph
Winston Churchill
Women in Space
Women of the Wild West
Yasser Arafat

ABOUT THE AUTHOR

Katherine Krohn is the author of many books for children and young adults, including award-winning biographies, fiction, and books on contemporary issues. She is a fan of Shakira and admires both her talent and humanitarian work. Krohn lives in the Pacific Northwest.

PHOTO ACKNOWLEDGMENTS

The images in this book are used with the permission of: © Frazer Harrison/Getty Images, p. 2; AP Photo/Fernando Vergara, p. 6; © Kimberly White/Getty Images, p. 9; © Gary Hershorn/Reuters/CORBIS, p. 11; © Alexander Pena/epa/CORBIS, p. 13; © Jeremy Horner/CORBIS, p. 14; © JP Laffont/Sygma/CORBIS, p. 22; © Charles Bonnay/Time & Life Pictures/Getty Images, p. 26; © Omar Bechara Baruque; Eye Ubiquitous/CORBIS, p. 28; © Ray Tamarra/Getty Images, p. 32; AP Photo/Amy E. Conn, p. 36; © Piero Pomponi/Getty Images, p. 38; © Roberto Schmidt/AFP/Getty Images, p. 40; © Theo Wargo/WireImage.com, p. 42; © Scott Gries/Getty Images, pp. 44, 86; © Kevin Winter/Getty Images, p. 48; © Michael Caulfield/WireImage.com, p. 50; © DYN-Greco/Getty Images, p. 55; © Reuters/CORBIS, p. 57; © Steve Sands/New York Newswire/CORBIS, p. 58; © Adrian Dennis/epa/CORBIS, p. 63; © Lawrence Lucier/Getty Images, p. 65; © Carlos Alvarez/Getty Images, p. 66; © Robert Sullivan/AFP/Getty Images, p. 68; © Daniel Munoz/Reuters/CORBIS, p. 71; © Nancy Kaszerman/ZUMA Press, p. 74; © Frank Micelotta/Getty Images, p. 76; © Action Press/ZUMA Press, p. 80; AP Photo/Arnulfo Franco, p. 82; AP Photo/William Fernando Martinez, p. 90; © epa/CORBIS, p. 93; © Mike Nelson/epa/CORBIS, p. 95.

Front Cover: © Andrew Marks/Retna Ltd. Back Cover: © Roberto Schmidt/AFP/Getty Images.